TRICKY DICK'S
TACKLE BOX

DICK E. WILSON

iUniverse, Inc.
Bloomington

Tricky Dick's Tackle Box

iUniverse books may be ordered through booksellers or by contacting:

iUniverse
1663 Liberty Drive
Bloomington, IN 47403
www.iuniverse.com
1-800-Authors (1-800-288-4677)

ISBN: 978-1-4759-2576-0 (sc)
ISBN: 978-1-4759-2577-7 (ebk)

Printed in the United States of America

iUniverse rev. date: 05/23/2012

DEDICATION

The short stories contained in this book are but a few of the memorable fishing trips I have been in during the past forty years, while fishing the waters of the beautiful Gulf of Mexico with family and friends. This book is dedicated to my life long mate and beautiful wife, Jacqueline and our immediate family, our five children; Steve, Kim, Kris, Mike and Marty, plus our eleven grandchildren; Mary Lee, Blake, Nick, Jordan, Tori, David, Jessica, Katie, Myia, Jett and Jace. "A family that fishes together, stays together." My mantra has always been to "Take a Kid Fishing!" DEW

CONTENTS

ACKNOWLEDGMENTS

Where would I be without my fantastic family and wonderful friends? This book is made up from a part of my life spent in Biloxi on the beautiful Mississippi Gulf Coast about family and friends that have enriched my life this past 40 years. To acknowledge everyone that have been a part of this book would be impossible, however, I do want to praise and thank those that made it possible. First and foremost, is my lifetime companion; love of my life; my fantastic and beautiful wife of 58 years, Jacky. It is through her genuine love, thoughtfulness and being the person she is, that I continue to praise God for providing me with such great life we share. She is the driving force that made this book and its' journal of personal fishing experiences possible. For nearly six months, she and our talented family friend and long time employee at Art F/X Studio Gallery, Penny Shirey, have worked diligently using their God given talents in compiling, editing and following up on the completion of this book. There are so many members of my family, great friends and fishing buddies that have contributed to this book and I thank each of you. I must acknowledge my father, the late Charles R. Wilson, who started me fishing at the early age of three. Not only did he introduce me and teach me the art and technique of fishing, but also the importance of marine life conservation. I too have had the pleasure of spending over 50 years of fishing with my own children, Steve, Kimberly, Kristina, Mike and Marty. Of course, as the years have gone by, my beautiful daughters found their "Soul-mates', moved on and have children of their own, that I also have the pleasure of fishing with periodically. My three sons have continued to be close fishing buddies. Today they are also ardent fishermen and teaching others the values and joys of this great outdoor sport. I must add by saying simply that God has given me a wonderful family and many friends. Each has taught me to believe and cherish life and look forward to the hereafter to join His "Fishermen of Men?

PREFACE

Seems that everybody has a good ol' Buddy. Golfing; Fishing; Bowling; Tennis; Jogging; Sailing; Drinking; Boating; Traveling; Swimming; Diving; Flying and so on. And, that's not too bad. It gives one the opportunity to share, learn and enjoy the things we have in common with our friends and family. I know I have been blessed with "buddies" of all ages, interest and intelligence. And as the years go by, our interests, abilities, desires, goals and capabilities change allowing us to spend more time doing what we enjoy most and with whom.

After years of enjoying a highly active life, playing sports, driving race cars and flying high performance aircraft, I realize that I have slowed down somewhat and that fishing has moved to my number one activity. Even though I have been an active angler for well over 75 years, at 82 years old, I am still a student in learning all the what, where, when and how about life. This includes the art of fishing. Every fishing trip that I take I learn something, from my sons, family members and all the wonderful buddies I have fished with throughout the years. My Father was my first fishing buddy, (along with my Uncle Frank.) When one couldn't take me, usually the other would. Then came grade school, high school and college and fishing was still a great pass time. From the rivers to the many beautiful lakes throughout northern Indiana, many a fish was taken while fishing with a couple of my classmates and early fishing buddies, Bob Truitt and Darl Caley. (Both now deceased) However, sports and members of the opposite sex came into my life, and I didn't fish with the interest I had before. Eventually, I found my life long buddy, my wife of 57 years, Jacky. After college and marriage, we soon became an Air Force family. Our family increased and soon I had a new "Buddy", Steve, the first born of our five children. At the age of three, we started a lifetime of fishing together. Then, in the late '50s, along came our two daughters, Kim and Kris and in 1962 we were blessed with twin boys, Mike and Marty. During the mid 60's, while stationed out of Las Vegas, we fished as a family on Lake Mead and the Colorado River whenever I was home. By 1966, Mike and Marty joined their older brother Steve as fishing buddies. As an Air Force Fighter Pilot, I spent a lot of time TDY, however during the next several years while stationed at Kadina AFB in Okinawa, we spent many hours fishing and diving in the East China Sea. During this time I also spent another tour in Vietnam. The war in Vietnam was coming to a halt, in 1972, we were assigned to Keesler AFB, Biloxi, Ms. My first "real" ground job. So, I bought a boat and fishing returned as my number one pass time again. By this time, I had three built in fishing buddies and yet, as a family, we went fishing, Floundering and crabbing every time we got a chance. Of course, I soon found new adult fishing buddies, as the boys not only had school, but also other "interests". My first local fishing mentor was Capt. Bud Patronas, a Charter boat Captain of the "Miss Ossie". Even though the boys and I fished the "Back Bay" every chance we had, Bud started me fishing the Mississippi Sound and I soon bought my own "out front" boat. And, as the years past, I acquired some great fishing buddies, some of which I still fish with, some 35 years later. Some however, are no longer with us. Grady Cook, Col. Dick Davis, John Lambeth, Toxie Smith and Ralph Hyer, were five wonderful fishing buddies, and from each I learned so much and truly miss them today. Yes, I also fished with my father-in law, the late Charlie Smith and my four brother-in-laws, Chuck Smith, the late Michael Smith, Larry Smith and my sisters' husband, the late Gordon Thrasher. Each, I considered a family fishing buddy. And even though I have my boys as life-time fishing buddies, I have been so very fortunate during the past 39 years to have some other great fishing buddies, past and present and many still living here on the Coast. To mention a few that I have fished with the most: Dick Hoover, Mike Chester, Steve Muench, Ray Lenaz, Les Terrell, Mike Suarez, George Junket, Terry Stewert, Kerry Hestler, Bill Boutwell, Glenn Breminkamp, Ronnie and Brittany Blacklidge, Harvey Nixon, and Michael Peterson. Here again, I continue to learn and place great value in having this great group of Fishing Buddies.

WINTER MULLETING

The date was, January 1977. The time: 0900 hours. The place: Biloxi Back Bay, on the beautiful Mississippi Gulf Coast. It was an extremely cold morning, as during the night, the temperature had dropped well below freezing. The windows were layered with icy crystals, making it difficult to really see the wintry scene that Mother Nature had produced. It appeared that, other than right down the center of the channel, the entire Back Bay was now covered with a layer of thin ice. Man, I could hardly believe my eyes!! Even the grass, that separated our house from the waters edge, was covered with tiny, sparkling saber blades that shimmered in the sun as the cold wind blew briskly out of the North. Having retired from the United States Air Force in 1976, I had become involved in catching up with all those things that I never seemed to have time to do. I guess, one never ever really gets caught up, but right then, I just wanted to do something different. Even though, it had not been real cold, up until now, it was still cold enough to make it uncomfortable to spend much time on the water. I had already cleaned and lubricated most of my fishing gear and restocked my tackle box for the new fishing year ahead. So, bored and suffering from "Cabin Fever", I called my old retired military and fishing buddy, (now the late, Col. Dick Davis, who retired a year before I did), and when he answered, I quickly asked, "O.K. Richard, just what do you do on the first winter after retirement and it's too damn cold to go fishing???" "Hey there Tricky Dick," he replied, "What's on your mind this beautiful morning? Have you looked outside yet'?" I told him I had and how amazed I was with what I saw." I was looking through my little "peep-hole" at the same time, and all at once, I realized I was looking at something that I had not noticed before. I quickly opened the sliding patio door to get a clearer look and leaned our as far as the phone cord would allow me. To my amazement, there were literally hundreds of fish all along the shoreline and on the thin layer of ice. There were even more, poking their heads up through the ice, to get oxygen. The channel was covered with fish as far as the eye could see.

There were Sheepshead, White Trout, Specks, Redfish, and tons of Popeye Mullet everywhere! Most of the fish that were coming up through the ice were MULLET! Realizing that I was quite cold by this time, I quickly retreated back into the house.

I related to Dick what I was witnessing and told him that I would call him right back. I then dialed the Marine Research Laboratory in Ocean Springs and asked to talk to a marine biologist. That being done, I explained what had happened and what would cause such a phenomena? He assured me that it was just one of those rare freaks of nature where the oxygen in the water is so low from the layer of ice that the fish actually suffocate. I then ask him if the fish were still all right to eat and he informed me that as long as they were still alive, they would be fine, however, not knowing how long others had been dead, he would not advise eating them. I thanked him, and called Dick back to relate our conversation. Then, I ask him if he might be interested in a few Mullet, as there were live ones all over the place and my little skiff was on the bank and I just needed to put a couple of paddles in and we would be in business. He must have also been very bored, as I received a resounding reply, "Let's go for it! I will be right over." After I hung up the phone, I got to thinking about what I had just said about being, "in business". Well, the next phone call was to a seafood dealer that I had heard always bought Mullet, or "Biloxi Bacon", as Mullet have been commonly referred to here for years. I dialed the first name I found in the book and asked if they were interested in buying some fresh Mullet. "Well, maybe. How many 'ya got'?" I quickly told him that we had a lot of them and he said, "Bring 'em on over and I'll take a look at 'em". Then ask, how much would he pay? And he quickly replied, ".16 cents a pound". Well, that sounded kind'a low to me for this time a year, so I thanked him and looked for another dealers' number. This time I came right to the point and ask, "Sir, how much do you pay a pound for fresh Mullet this time of year?" He replied, "Well, if their real fresh and not all black bellied, I'll pay the same as I do buying out of Florida." "And how much is that Sir," I quickly ask! ".26 cents a pound and not a penny more." He replied. I advised him that they were very fresh. Some were even still alive and were not caught around any of the seafood processing factories.

By the time that Dick got to my house, I had the boat in the water and the little motor mounted and ready to go. Thinking ahead, I had also put a couple of fish landing nets in the boat so that if possible we could just scoop 'em up as we moved through the water. Wow! It worked like a charm. As my little skiff moved through the water it broke the thin layer of ice and exposed hundreds of Mullet moving slowly just below the surface. I grabbed one of the landing nets and made a quick dip and before I realized it, the net was so full of fish that I could hardly lift it into the boat. Seeing that, Dick quickly grabbed the other net and went to work on the other side of the boat. For the next fifteen minutes we were busy filling the boat with Mullet. As a matter of fact, it was so full, that if either one of us were to lean over to make another scoop, we would have surely swamped. When we arrived at the dock, I ran to the garage and brought back one of my 172 Qt. igloo coolers and we quickly loaded it to the brim with just Mullet.

When we arrived at the seafood market place, the owner was there to meet us and the first thing he did was have his helpers cut the bellies to see if they were nice and clear. Usually, Mullet found around the processing plants tend to have a real black inside lining and even have a little unfavorable taste. Well, satisfied that they were good and fresh, he weighed out our catch, which came to over 200 pounds! That worked out to a little over $55.00! Not too bad for 15 minutes work, plus the transportation. I mentioned to him that there were plenty more where those came from and he said he could take at least another cooler full. So, home we went and were back within the hour with another cooler full of "beautiful" fresh Mullet. (And that would mean another $55.00) Wow! Nearly $115.00 so far and it wasn't even noon yet. Not to let a good thing pass us by, I quietly ask the owner how many more he could handle? He informed me that he felt this was it for the day. When I ask him about any other seafood dealers, he kind'a scratched his head and ask if we would take .22 cents a pound for another 400 pounds? "Of course," was my quick response and we headed back to the house. Another quick drag or two through the channel and boat was again dangerously full. This time, Dick had brought along his 172 Qt. cooler and rather than make two trips, we just filled up another cooler and headed down the road. As we approached the loading dock, I could not help but notice that the seafood dealers' truck, from the first dealer that I had called and was offered .16 cents a pound, was backed up to the dock. Well, you guessed it! He was there to buy the Mullet from the dealer that we were selling it to. "Course, we could care less, as we were happy with our deal. As we were leaving, I couldn't help but wonder how much he was paying. It's really ironic that we would have taken even .20 cents a pound if the first dealer would have offered, and now we knew that he was paying at least .22 cents a pound. I did find out later that he paid .24 cents a pound. Later that afternoon, after we cleaned up our mess and put everything away, we counted our profits and came up with $202.55! Split down the middle, that came to over $101.00 each! Not bad for a couple of old retired Air Force Pilots. And what did I do with the money? Probably bought a new rod and reel, like I really needed one.

FISHING THE PIERS AND BRIDGES

To many Mississippi Gulf Coast fishermen, a pier or a bridge is just a man-made structure jutting out over the water to be used to fish on when a boat is not available and the urge to weta line is just over-powering. Wow! What a mouth full! But the point is, to many other anglers these piers and old bridges do offer a whole world of fishing excitement. From Alabama to Louisiana, hundreds of piers and old bridges just out over some of the most potent shallow water fishing grounds on the Mississippi Gulf Coast, including many of the beautiful bays and bayous. They vary in length, height, type structure and importance as to location and accessibility. But one component all have in common is the opportunity for large numbers of people to enjoy some fine fishing at minimal cost. Most of the old bridges are maintained by, the local city, county, or state as a recreational site. Many are structurally modified so the fishermen can drive out on the structure and park right next to the spot from which he wants to fish, without having to walk a country mile while carrying an ice chest, bait, rods and reels and other fishing gear. One very popular drove-on bridge on the Mississippi Coast is the old Biloxi-Ocean Springs bridge located at the very eastern end of Howard Avenue, on Point Cadet in Biloxi. This old fishing bridge is the longest free fishing pier in the state, jutting out into the mouth of the historic Biloxi Back Bay for just over one mile. It also has been modified so as to provide a turn-around at the very end. For years it has been a favorite fishing spot for family outings as well as for the ardent fisherman. Most species taken daily from these piers and old bridges may be classified as saltwater marine pan-fish. Of course, most saltwater fishermen would not agree that their favorite catch in shallow water is anything near a pan-fish, however, compared to the great King Mackerel, Cobia, Jack-Cravelle, Bonito, Bull Red and Black Drum, they appear quite small. Common species taken from the average pier or bridge fisherman are: Speckled Trout, White Trout, Drum, Ground Mullet, Rat Reds, Flounder, Sheephead and Croaker. However, one can not become too complacent while fishing for the smaller species, for at any time, day or night, especially in the fall of the year, a bruising tackle-buster may choose your bait for his meal, and the fight is on. Many a trophy-size catch has been made from a pier or bridge and many a monster has been lost. Black Drum, weighing over 50 pounds, Bull Reds, over 30 pounds, Sheephead, up to 15 pounds and even Speckled Trout in the 7 pound class have been reported. Although many pier and bridge fishermen are bottom fishermen and have a knack of telling what specie is biting, many are still surprised when the battle is over and their prize comes to the surface. One never really knows just what monster of the deep the deep might come along. I guess that's why sometimes it looks like they have too heavy a tackle for the size fish they normally catch. Better to be safe then sorry, if you hook the big one. Many pier and bridge fishermen prefer to use fresh shrimp, when in season, however, different species do have their favorite food source at different times of the year. For example, when White Trout or Ground Mullet are biting good, fresh squid is one of the most productive baits. Many a large Flounder have also been landed using just plain old cut bait. While fiddler crabs and small rock crabs are killers for Sheephead. Of course, some bait requires a little more work to find then others. Lots of fishermen prefer to use live bait over most all other baits and I happen to be one of those. I prefer live shrimp, small fish or bull minnows. They can be used to fish the bottom or one of the most popular methods is to use a weighted popping cork with the live bait dangling 18 inches to 3 to 4 feet below the cork. By executing sharp upward movements of the rod tip, the popping cork "pops" across the surface, jerking the bait in a forward and upward movement, simulating a frightened shrimp or minnow. When live bait is not available, artificial baits may be used in the same manner and often produce surprising results unless you have been talking to my friend Fred Deegen, who is never really surprised at what his artificial baits' will catch. One of the hardest fighting fish which many times will surprise the pier fishermen, regardless of what kind of bait he may be using, is the Sand Shark, Dog Fish or a Blacktip Shark. Though considered a non-edible fish by many of the uninformed, the Blacktipped Shark is every bit as palatable as many of the more desirable species when properly prepared. As a matter of fact, there are really very few shallow water species that are not edible. I have tried eating every type of non-poisonous fish that I have had the opportunity, and with a little seasoning and a strong stomach, I could survive if I had to . . . . I think!!! In addition to the hook and line fishermen, there is another very proficient and proud pier and bridge fishermen. Many a morning the old Biloxi-Ocean Springs

Bridge is crowded with the artistic cast-net fishermen, seeking their favorite species, the Popeye Mullet, better known around southern Mississippi as good old BILOXI BACON. Overcast days and early morning hours are prime times and as the sun begins to rise, the cast-netters are replaced by the hook and line fishermen, keeping the popular bridge a busy place most of the time. So if your one of those land-locked fishermen or just want a good place to take the family to go fish'n or crab'n, don't overlook the many piers and bridges available to you on the Mississippi Gulf Coast. Try it sometimes, it can be fun!!!

SNAKES AND FISHERMEN

As spring changes into summer, more and more sportsmen venture outdoors, resulting in an increased exposure to the many species of snakes that have come out of hibernation to enjoy the warming rays of the sun. Many a fishermen have routinely encountered these slithering serpents while in quest of one of man's favorite sports. Because of their historical portrayal as a dangerous and evil creature, snakes usually startle even the most experienced outdoorsmen, when suddenly encountered. And since some snakes are venomous and can be hazardous to our very existence, this stimulation of man's adrenalin may well be justified. It should be noted however, that of the 40 species of snakes found in Mississippi, only 6 species are poisonous to man and at least two of these are not found through out the entire state. The 6 poisonous species found in Mississippi are the cottonmouth, copperhead, eastern diamondback rattlesnake, pygmy rattlesnake, timber rattlesnake and the eastern coral snake. The first 5 species are "Pit Vipers" and their bite is hemotoxic, while the coral snake does not have the pit vipers two fangs, and their bite is neurotoxic. Most experienced outdoorsmen are able to identify the poisonous species and unless it is a sudden encounter, have little concern when they cross paths. A true outdoor sportsman usually will, neither, injure or kill a snake in their natural environment, in that they realize that they are very important in natures balance. Since no one wants to be bitten, especially by a poisonous snake, it is well to give all snakes proper respect. Even experienced outdoorsmen have been bitten through carelessness.

In general, the creek, river and pond fishermen have the greatest exposure to snakes, primarily because at one time or another, most of these species inhabit these areas near some type of water source. The cottonmouth is no doubt the most commonly found, however, the rattlesnake and coral snake may also be around damp swampy areas near other bodies of water. The copperhead is usually found in the woodlands, rock and log, strewn hillsides, and sometimes in areas of heavy brush along the edge of swampy marches and bayous. Even the saltwater fisherman must remain alert when bank fishing or fishing along, rocky jetties. I know for a fact that cottonmouths and rattlesnakes may be found sunning themselves along the banks of saltwater inlets and along the sides of jetties. I can recall, one time while fishing off a long jetty early one morning along the Texas gulf coast, I decided to walk to the end of the jetty and see how the other fishermen were doing in the deeper water. Due to the wind and the direction of the tide, most of the fishermen were fishing on the same side of the jetty. As I slowly walked along the opposite side of the jetty, I was attracted by literally hundreds of fiddler crabs and sea lice that were scurrying for cover. Much to my surprise, I suddenly spotted a large cottonmouth neatly coiled just a scant six inches off the rocky path down the center of the jetty. He was in a loose, flat coil and gave no indication that I might be interrupting his nap in the warm sun. I carefully backed away from him and as I looked around, noticed that just on the other side of the jetty, not more than six or seven feet away, sat a man and two young boys, completely engrossed in their fishing. I quickly, but carefully advised them that they had some uninvited company and pointed out the deadly serpent. Before I could say anymore, or even attempt to stop him, the terrified father jumped up and promptly beat the snake to death with a, two foot club that seemed to appear from nowhere. Even though he fearlessly attacked the deadly pit viper, I could not help but notice that his hand was still shaking nervously as he held the now lifeless, 4 foot snake up for his sons to see. Not satisfied with this, he began to search the edge of the jetty for more and was rewarded by finding and killing 3 or more smaller cottonmouths within about 20 feet either side of where they were fishing. As we discussed the fact that evidently, it was still cool enough that even with the early morning sun, the snakes were still sluggish and inactive, he began to get his fishing gear together and advised the boys that he thought it was time to leave.

Another incident I remember well was while surf fishing at night for Bull Reds. During the late hours one fall evening, we had fished the first sand bar while we waited for the tide to drop so that we could get to the second bar without getting in over our head, we heard a yell from on shore. Looking up, we saw that the jeep lights were on and someone was blasting the horn. It was not uncommon for someone to run up and move the jeep every once in a while as the group proceeded to fish down the beach, but this time there seemed to be something wrong. As we quickly responded and moved toward the jeep, the driver motioned for us to come around the side of the vehicle. He then pointed out a large snake coiled on the beach, directly in front of the jeep, clearly visible in the jeeps headlights. One of the group found a sturdy piece of driftwood to use as a club and slowly advanced toward the snake, careful not to enter the beam of light from the headlights. As we all drew closer, we were surprised to see that the large snake looked like a western diamondback rattlesnake. Feeling the vibrations, the snake had already coiled and even above the roar of the nearby surf, you could make out his spine-chilling rattle. Our fishing companion with the club moved cautiously to within striking distance, while remaining outside the beam of light. As he attempted to deliver a lethal blow to the head, the snake suddenly moved just as the club came into the beam of light. While missing the intended target, the club did deliver a crippling blow about one-third of the way down the body causing the snake to strike out at the club, and then gather into a tight coil with its body nearly covering its head. It eventually took several, well placed blows to the head to fully subdue the angry and fatally wounded snake. Fortified with this startling event, we all became more cautious about where we walked and by the time night had turned into morning, we had encountered 4 more rattlesnakes along the beach. Not quite as large but just as dangerous, we kept our distance from them and they slithered off the beach to the protective darkness.

During the past 40 years of fishing and hunting, I have encountered hundreds of snakes and have learned to be ever alert and to give these creatures proper respect. Not just through fear, but also for their place in our world. It is really you who are invading their world, so if at all possible, make the effort to go around and usually the snake will go in the opposite direction. Many times, while setting Trout lines or frog hunting late at night, I have come dangerously close to nearly camouflaged serpents before spotting them almost too late. This is especially true of the cottonmouth. He gives no warning and will set, dead still, nearly invisible, waiting for his dinner. That you happen to interrupt his evening can both alarm him and make him angry. Keep a sharp look out, especially at night. To say which species is the most dangerous or which has the most lethal poison would open "Pandora's box", as there are countless contributing factors which can vary with time of year, geographic location, age and size of the snake and the amount of poison extracted. The important thing is to be fully aware that a poisonous snake can be anywhere and during spring and summer, it is easy to become complacent and careless while engrossed in fishing near some of those most likely hiding spots. In conclusion, remember, not all snakes are harmful and they do have a place in natures delicate balance. No matter where you fish, be alert to the fact that some places are more conducive to harboring snakes than others. We know for a fact that the typical fisherman can be found everywhere in quest of one of man's favorite sports, and this can bring SNAKES AND FISHERMEN together.

FISHING AND BOATING ETHICS

How many times have you felt frustration, hostility and even hate because some inconsiderate, selfish individual ruined your whole days outing? Too many people living right here in Mississippi, as well as in other parts of the South, violate the moral and ethical rights of other outdoorsmen. I find` this especially true on the water. Sport fishermen, commercial fishermen, shrimpers, pleasure boaters, water sport enthusiasts and even swimmers are many times not given mutual respect while participating in their specialty. Usually, the so-called "WEEKEND WARRIOR' receives 90% of the blame when a boat blunders into sacred Fishing grounds, nearly swamping any smaller skiffs at anchor, or he may noisily throw his anchor overboard, directly over the very spot you were fishing. But, when the truth is known, there are far more "WATER-BULLIES", which include experienced fishermen, who think that they have the right to that space of water, no matter who's there first. Another group of spoilers are mixed in with the "WATER SPORT ENTHUSIASTS." This includes reckless skiers, inconsiderate scuba divers, dangerous pleasure boaters and even some sail boaters. We all realize that, this assorted group of unethical slobs, are only a small percentage of the typical outdoorsmen we meet on the water, for they are that minor group of selfish, thick-headed, individuals that are persistently ruining things for the majority. For the benefit of those who fall into the minority group of spoilers, but may not realize it, lets take a look at an example of each of the above, mentioned types.

"WEEKEND WARRIORS"—Many times we inadvertently label the everyday working man, who because of his job can only get out on the weekends, a "Weekend Warrior." We tend to do this mainly because of a few individuals who seldom get on the water, have purchased a high-powered speed hull and, due to their lack of experience and practical knowledge of the "rules of the road", often find themselves the center of attention. Unaware of the detrimental effect of their rolling wake at low to medium speeds, they plow their crafts dangerously close to other boats including small fishing skiffs at anchor, nearly capsizing them. The stigma placed upon the weekend fishing and boating enthusiast is really not quite fair to the average individual, for here again, it is only that small percentage that are so totally ignorant.

"WATER BULLIES"—Here we find a few sport fishermen and a few commercial fishermen, including the everyday recreational fishermen, shrimpers, crabbers, etc., who basically know better, but appear to not really care what harm or hostility they create by their selfish actions. They seem to feel that since they are on the water everyday, and for many it's their livelihood, that they have special rights. Such as, since the shortest distance between two points is a straight line, they have the right to steer straight up the middle of a group of small fishing skiffs or to cruise between the shore line and a skiff at anchor fishing toward that very shoreline. This action, not only, normally spooks the fish, especially in fairly shallow water, but can also create a wake problem if not at idle speed. Another "water bully" is the so called super-sportsman that, after watching the occupants of the other boats catching fish after fish, he maneuvers his boat so as to locate himself directly over the very spot the fish were being caught. Many times the noise, movement of the water and crowded conditions can either disrupt the feeding or most often will spook the fish completely for the day.

"WATER-SPORT ENTHUSIAST"—This group is a conglomeration of various fun seekers. The water skier seems to head the list of irritates to the fishermen, as they can be most frustrating on small bodies of water, particularly in the bayous and small bays. The noise and repeated surface activity cannot help but have a very detrimental effect on the feeding of most game fish being sought. This coupled with the constant rocking of the skiff as a result of the frequent passing to the ski boat becomes an insurmountable irritant. In confined areas of relatively small bodies of water, there is very little that can be done, if the boats are legally allowed to be there. On large bodies of water, even though the skier had every bit as much right to be there as anyone else, certain ethics should certainly apply. I can even understand why many times fishermen are harassed by skiers when they are anchored way back in a cove where the water is nice and calm because this is where they like to ski, however, with so many other areas of water for them to use, it is really hard to accept. A new water sport enthusiast is the jet-skier . . . . !This speeding daredevil can really play with your temper as he cuts in and out of the various tributaries that so often are a Trout fisherman's paradise and demand tranquility. Things really get hectic when a group of jet skiers start playing "chicken" or "water tag" anywhere near you. In general, most jet-skiers are very careful not to disturb others, however, once again there are always those few that spoil things.

Another water-sport enthusiast that can really raise havoc with the deepwater fishermen is the scuba diver. Here again, the spear gun fisherman has just a much right to be down there on top of that reef or wreak as the surface fisherman has to be over the top of it. The real conflict comes into play over respect for whoever was their first. If the diver is there first, he feels that he has squatters rights and really could care less what goes on top side as long as they don't hit him with an anchor or snag him with a set of treble hooks. They usually have their area marked off well with divers floats and are careful to stay clear of the surface fishermen. On the other hand, the surface fisherman is very offended and usually becomes quite hostile if, while fishing over his favorite wreck, a boat load of scuba divers pull right up beside him and a bunch of divers jump overboard directly into the area that his is fishing. Most of the time, once the fish get used to the new arrivals, they move around again and will feed in a relatively normal manner. But again, there are always a few who look for trouble such as the prankster who will swim over and jerks down on the surface fisherman's line, simulating a bite. This childish and frustrating trick is enough by itself, but it stands to reason that no other creature can or will bite while this type activity is going on around the bait. Then, on the other hand, there are always a few thoughtless surface fishermen that will race up to their old fishing spot and throw out the anchor without paying any attention to the divers buoy. These acts of unsportsmanship are not only extremely inconsiderate but can also be very dangerous.

"PLEASURE BOATERS"—Reckless boat drivers are a danger to everyone on or in the water. Even small speed hulls zig-zagging in and out of the bayous and bays where other water enthusiasts are playing or fishing creates a hazardous and many times frustrating situation. Many times boats with the right-of-way must alter their course to prevent a collision with a fast moving pleasure boat whose driver appears to think they are the only ones on the water. Large luxury boats, which create monstrous wakes at low speeds, can make things both exciting and dangerous for the smaller vessels. Many a small boat has been capsized from the wake of a larger boat. Even though you would not know it to watch some boaters, all boat operators are responsible for their wake and should be very aware of its impact upon other boats, even those at dock side.

"SAILBOATERS"—Here is a group of water sport enthusiast that have almost all the "rules of the road" in their favor when under sail, because of their dependency on the wind for movement and maneuverability. However, they too are abused many times by all types of watercraft whose drivers do not realize just how vulnerable a sailboat is at times. On the other hand, it is very difficult to keep from becoming upset when along comes a sailboat in wide-open waters, and passes within a few feet of your small, anchored Fishing skiff. I have even had them catch my lines in their free board or tiller. And then to make matters even worse, they continue on as if they have never even seen you as they take all the line from your reels. That is if the line doesn't break first or jerk your rod overboard. Even with just 10 to 15 feet clearance, they could prevent this from happening. But, they feel that they have the right-of-way because of being under sail. As sophisticated as they appear, they can also be another type of water bully.

Yes, there are many violations of rights and ethics on the water by a few selfish and irresponsible slobs, however each type of water participant are in general courteous and careful and respect the rights of others. But, every time you are on the water, ask yourself if you are one of the majority or one of the above, mentioned minorities? Be aware of your Boating and Safety Ethics.

LATE FALL FISHING

The first cold blast of winter hit early in the fall of 1983, with the temperature dropping into the low fifties along the Mississippi Gulf Coast. Fishermen that weathered the chilly morning wind during the later part of September, were rewarded with sudden increased catches of White Trout, Rat Reds, Flounder and Ground Mullet while fishing the shell beds around piers, old bridges and jetties. More wade fishermen on the front beach emerge from the cooling waters of the Gulf with respectable catches of Speckled Trout. October and November are historically great fishing months for the gulf coast fishermen and this late fall should be no exception. For those who seldom have the opportunity to go fishing by boat and have to depend upon the fish coming to them along the shoreline while fishing from the piers and jetties, this is their time of year. Almost every kind of shallow water species are caught until the water temperature drops down into the low sixties. Many a novice angler may fill their coolers during a single days outing, just fishing from the shore, should they hit the right time of day. Of course, those fortunate enough to have a boat may even have more success, due to accessibility to the various "hot spots" that can only be reached by boat. Stands to reason that if you can go to the fish instead of having to wait for the fish to come to you, your chances are much better. As a bait camp owner, I am frequently quizzed as to what is the best bait to use that day. Frankly, unless I have talked to someone fishing that day or I have just gone myself, I don't really know, because the "best bait" can change from day to day and many times from one hour to the next. Of course, I usually know what they were hitting on the day before and about what time and that does give us a starting point. I'm sure that most "Speck" fishermen agree that as long as live shrimp are available, it is the most productive bait for Speckled Trout. Normally, during the fall and early winter months, squid and cut bait are excellent for White Trout and Ground Mullet and I have seen many times that it was preferred even over shrimp. The type of fish that you are planning to go after has a lot to do with the bait selection. Many times I have departed the dock with my sons, fully intending to make a whole day of it fishing as many of my favorite "hot spots" as time would allow. Therefore, we would take, an ample supply of each of the above, mentioned baits. We usually start by hunting for Specks with live shrimp and systematically move from spot to spot until we hit them or strike out. Before the sun is too high, we are anchored over one of our favorite Red Fish, Ground Mullet or White Trout reefs, experimenting with the various baits we have with us while basically bottom fishing. If nothing great materializes within the next 20-30 minutes, we move on to another honey hole. But, if the fishing is average or better, we continue to stick with it, using whatever bait is the most productive. We have found that the oyster reefs are the most productive during the fall months, especially during a strong changing tide. It is not uncommon to hook into a 20 to 30 pound Bull Red, as on one highly productive trip, I landed five beautiful Bull Reds in less than an hours time along with a great catch of White Trout and Ground Mullet. There are many old and newly formed reefs located right here along our own Mississippi coast, that are not open to oystering all year, but are available and accessible to fishermen in small skiffs, providing the seas are fairly calm. As the late fall Speck fishing reaches a peak, live shrimp may become scarce and even the early morning fishermen frequently have difficulty finding live bait. Other substitutes for live shrimp are bull minnows and the small "Pogie" or Menhaden. On several occasions I have fished side by side with another angler who was using live Menhaden and been out fished. However, fishing with live Menhaden does have some drawbacks. In the first place, to the best of my knowledge, few, if any bait camps ever have Menhaden. That means that you have to use Braille net and get your own bait. Next, it is common knowledge that they are more difficult to keep alive. By late fall, bull minnows are usually more available than shrimp or Menhaden, but not really as good a Speck bait. I should add that they are really great for Flounder. Until the water gets too cool, most wade-fishermen use live shrimp or their favorite artificial Speck killer. Off shore Speck fishermen, working the islands and marshes usually prefer artificial baits primarily due to the difficulty of keeping the shrimp alive when having to travel so far to fish, plus the simplicity of just carrying a tackle box. Mirro-lures, Bingos, Speck rigs, Trout-tails, Speck tails and a host of other jigs, grubs and spoon type lures may be used on any given day with equal success. Here again, the Speck and Red Fishing can be hot and heavy during these cool fall months and many an island trip has produced highly respectable catches.

Another technique still used by many "never-say-die" Speck fishermen, is to slowly troll the deep holes up the bays bayous and rivers once the water temperatures have dropped into the mid fifties. Those fortunate enough to find a few large live shrimp, usually have the best chance of catching the "big ones". Bull minnows, fished in this manner can also be productive as a second choice or even as a last resort for some prefer to use their favorite artificial lure. As the fall fades into winter, and there is no live bait available, you may still see the old timers still catching a few everyday, while lazily trolling back and forth over their hot spot with their lucky Speck lure.

So, if you haven't had a chance to break away from you busy schedule and relax at your favorite sport during this past summer, now's an excellent time to still get with it and catch up. The weather may be a little cooler and some days not quite as comfortable as you might like, but the chances for anyone and everyone to catch fish are above average. Once the water temperature drops below 50 degrees however, things get pretty grim in the shallow water fish'n department and it starts getting time to fix up, oil up, clean up and put up our fishing gear for a month or two 'cause the majority of the so called saltwater pan fish have done moved to warmer water. Real LATE FALL FISHING inshore is not anything to get excited about, But come springtime, things start to pick up and I hope you'll be ready to "Take a Kid Fish'n"!!!!!

LUCKY OR GOOD

Looking back at the past 81 years, I could tell you a thousand fishing stories, and never tell a story the same way twice. "Course, ya gott'a be careful not to tell the same one twice if'n it's just a tall fish "tail." Ya see the difference between a fish "story" and a fish "tail" is usually in the numbers like, "how many?" or "how big?" and "where did ja catch'em?" When you repeat a fish "tail", you got to remember the numbers and the facts you used the first time and so on. However, when you relate a fish "story", you know the numbers and the real facts! I relate honest to goodness real fish stories, (most of the time), but, like some fishermen, I guess a little fish, "tail", might creep in when I get to bragg'n about my catch.

Well, anyway, even after hearing a few of my fish "stories", some of my friends think that I'm pretty LUCKY, while some think maybe I might be GOOD. For years, lots of folks have called me "LUCKY". They have accused me of catching fish while I was eat'n, sleep'n, swimm'n, boat'n, or even when answering the call of nature. In other words—they think I catch more fish by shear dumb LUCK than most people do with skill and practice. And ya know what? 'Maybe their right! Sometimes . . . kinda . . . . sorta . . . , maybe . . . . in some respects, in that I am LUCKY for sure. But then, there are other folk I fish with, that think I'm pretty good. And sometimes, their right too. Well, kinda, sorta, and as a matter of fact, maybe their both right. That is, I really think that anyone that goes fish'n a lot should catch fish more often than not! It's not really because they are so good, even though most agree that practice makes one better at most things. Nor is it that they are just plain LUCKY, because the law of average would soon catch up. It's logical that, as a result of fishing more than the average person, we tend to stay current as to what species are being caught, where they are being caught, what they are biting on and what is the best time of day to fish. First hand knowledge, acquired on a daily basis, does help to keep up with what is going on with our finny-friends, and will help to make one an above average angler. Then, of course, with a little LUCK sprinkled in with the above, it can really make it look like some folks are just plain LUCKY. Yes, everyone needs a little LUCK, no matter how, good a fishermen they may be, but, REMEMBER, nothing beats frequency! You got to go to catch!! The fish will not come knock'n at your door. You know, most fishermen never talk about the times that they got skunked or didn't catch enough to stink the skillet. But, that's O.K. as it can happen to anyone. When I do catch fish, I don't mind being called LUCKY, 'cause sometimes it might be true, maybe . . . . kinda . . . . sorta . . . . well, the proof is in the long term fish'n "story". Are you LUCKY or GOOD???

RAYS; SPORT, FOOD OR NUISANCE

Most fishermen from coast to coast regard the Ray somewhat of a dangerous nuisance when caught while fishing and usually just want to get rid of it as quickly as possible. However, such is not the case in some other parts of the world. For example, in Europe and England, the Ray is considered a tasty food fish. Having fished the shores of both the Atlantic and Pacific Oceans and the Gulf of Mexico from the Florida Keys to the Mexican boarder, I have caught virtually every kind of Ray found in the waters surrounding our nation. This even includes a very large Manta Ray, which I snagged by accident, and I had absolutely no control over it. I kept hoping that it would break the line or throw the hook, but after it stripped off every bit of the line, it almost jerked the rod out of my hand before the line finally did break. For many years I got rid of the intruder just a quickly as I could and thought nothing of cutting the line as close to the pancake shaped Ray as I dared. Then I heard several different stories and even read about seafood places accused of preparing stamped out Stingray and selling it for scallops. But, try as I might, I have never been able to confirm this, by personally seeing it done. But, this did arouse my interest in Rays as a food source. I really never had a chance to even check this out until about 15 years ago, while fishing along the eastern coast, I caught a big ole' 28 pound Cow Ray. Remembering all that I had heard about Rays, as a seafood, I cleaned it as best I knew how and stuck it in my cooler along with the fish. Actually, Rays are relatively easy to clean. Like Sharks, they have cartilage skeletons. In the center of each wing is a flexible cartilage with muscles on each side to make it move up and down. Filleting is as simple as cleaning a fish, by cutting down along the body as far as the cartilage and then cutting straight out along the wing to the tip. After cutting off the two fillets on the topside, the Ray is turned over and the same process repeated, producing a total of four nice triangles of meat. I had also read somewhere that it was best to cut each triangle into strips approximately an inch wide and then skin the strips, leaving the pretty white meat to be breaded and fried much like fried shrimp. I still fillet a Ray in this manner.

There are several ways to prepare a Ray as a great food source. The simplest is to wrap the filleted strips in a foil while smothered with butter and lime juice. For best results, it should be cooked at low temperature in a covered grill. The texture of a Ray is somewhat chewy, much like scallops but a bit milder flavored. By wrapping the strips in foil with the melted butter, it creates a steaming process that really enhances the Ray's mild flavor. Due to this mild flavor, it will pick up other flavors, such as hamburger, if you charcoal your Ray strips on a grill that has been recently used to grill hamburgers. I also read that left-over grilled Ray may be used as a Ray salad like tuna salad to make sandwiches and even can be used in a spaghetti sauce. Sometime I would like to try Ray fillet with Parmesan as I have heard that it was quite tasty. I do know for a fact that it is good smoked, even if it is a little chewy. In addition to being a tasty seafood when prepared properly, I have learned to respect most Rays as a fighter, once you get`em off the bottom, especially in deep water. They can really be a problem with light tackle. Large Rays either just move off and either break your line or just settle in and literally attach themselves to the bottom like an anchor with a suction cup attached. Rays will bite on almost any kind of dead bait just laying on the bottom, and many times will take a good live shrimp if you leave it in one place very long. Actually, a good size Ray will give a novice saltwater fishermen a real thrill and an exciting initiation to saltwater bottom fishing. Their runs are usually short, but just long enough and fast enough to require a steady rod and reel with a smooth drag. Then the strain of raising a Ray from the bottom and then controlling their runs as you bring them to the boat requires the combined use of drag and rod control. Once the Ray is tired and you have him along side the boat, he should be treated with respect for if handled improperly, he can ruin your whole day. Small Rays up to 10-15 pounds can usually be handled fairly easily with just a landing net and while being careful to stay clear of the tail barb, the hook can be disengaged and the Ray released. Larger Rays that can be used as a food source can be quickly put out of action with a hard smack with club. Be sure to remove the sharp barb on the tail by cutting it off with a sharp knife prior to cleaning the Ray. The spiny barb may be kept and dried out and bleached for use as a novelty letter opener. Simply file the small barbs off and should you desire, you can print the weight and date of catch on it prior to putting on a final finish. Any clear finish will usually work.

Rays on our Atlantic coast and the Gulf of Mexico are fairly plentiful. I have personally caught several dozen small Rays on a single outing and on many occasions while wade fishing, come up on a herd of Rays that covered several hundred feet of shoreline. Marine science and biology magazines have mentioned in several articles during the past few years, that large herds of Rays can cause considerable damage to shellfish beds and various marine advisory services have been exploring the idea of educating the public on the commercial market potential in an attempt to control their numbers. To date, nothing has been mentioned regarding this matter in the Gulf Coast waters.

So, remember, a Ray can be a dangerous nuisance as its spiny barb can inflict a serious and painful wound, however, it can also be a game fighter on light tackle and if prepared properly, a very tasty addition to your seafood menu. Have fun, but be careful and don't ever underestimate a Ray as sport, food or just a nuisance.

TIGHT-LINE FISHING

Day in, day out, season by season, tight-line fishing is the single most effective method for catching fish with a hook that has ever been devised throughout the world. From the muddy Mekong River in Southeast Asia to the clear cool waters of Canada, and especially throughout this great nation of ours, I have personally witnessed that more recreational fishermen use the "tight-line" method than any other. Realizing that one must take into account the fly fishermen, the bass fishermen and all of those folks that use a float of some sort, the number of anglers, young and old, rich and poor, amateur and experts, that tight-line still will out number all the rest. Tight-line rigs may be as simple as using a rusty old hook at the end of some kite string tied to willow branch and using a spark plug for a weight or as sophisticated, as you want by using expensive, near invisible mono-line, with special hooks, bright beads or spinners in front of the hook and with various types of weights located at strategic places. Tight-line rigs may be used with a combination rod and reel, a cane-pole, long limber branch or even used as just a hand line. Since tight-line fishing is such a broad subject and involves so many individual and personal techniques, depending what species of fish one may be trying to catch. I will limit this brief article to tight-line fishing with a long cane-pole, and lets say we want to specifically fish for Crappie or White Perch. It is common knowledge that during the fall months, Crappie fishermen seem to literally come out of the woodwork with their little skiffs, Coleman lanterns and all the associated gear for night Crappie fishing. As fall slides into winter, fewer and fewer lights may be seen across the water, even in our warmer states. However, during these late fall months, right here in southern Mississippi, there are places to go and fish to be caught using the tight-line method. Yes, tight-line fishing with minnows for bait has become very popular throughout all the southern states and still accounts for a large portion of the larger Crappie catches. It has become a rather standard method at a lot of the most popular and top Crappie hot spots located along the Mississippi River as well as on many of the lakes and rivers throughout the state. One very plus factor in favor of using the tight-line method is even the amateur angler can quickly learn to catch their share of Crappie, and it doesn't require a lot of expensive fishing gear. The most important thing to learn about tight-line fishing is the "feel". Meaning, to be able to detect strikes, especially when they are so very light. Folks with a delicate sense of feel pick up on this rapidly and even the amateur soon identify the slightest tap. Granted, the very easiest method is to watch a cork and when it goes down, you simply set the hook. However, this becomes more difficult in deep water and requires more sophisticated rigging. Now, just what is tight-line fishing, what kind of rig is used and do other fish bite when you're fishing for a specific species? Basically, tight-line fishing is simply keeping a tight line on your bait so that when the fish starts to eat or take the bait off the hook, the vibrations will be sent up the line, through the pole and be felt in your hands. If the line is not tight enough, you will not feel this action until the line does get tight and by then it might be too late. Most fishermen are familiar with tight-line bottom fishing, but there are still many who have never fished a tight line from a long pole and the magic to this is how it is used.

There are several variations to put a standard tight-line rig together, and most fishermen have his or her favorite way. Here again, the magic is not in the equipment, but how it is used. A very common rig used is even available through commercial outlets and is simply called a "Crappie rig". A very simple rig that can be homemade without the factory made wire drops. This rig uses about a 3 foot length of heavy line with a dipsey or bell sinker on the bottom. Above the sinker at about 12 inch intervals are drops for the hooks, tied so that each rides about 4 inches out from the main line, typical dropper style. A barrel swivel is usually attached at the top. An alternate rig uses a shorter piece of line with a slip sinker located about 8 inches above the hook that is tied at the bottom end. The second hook is tied near the other end with a drop like the first rig described. A barrel swivel may be used at the top. There are different requirements for the use, of a long cane-pole verses a spin-casting or bait-casting rod. The first type used for fishing shallower water, requires no reeling device and the total length of line, including the rig is no longer then the pole itself. Under some circumstances, it may be lengthened or shortened as desired for the depth of water your fishing. Works well fishing from shore or boat. The other method when fishing deep water, is using a rod and reel and can be let down 20 or 30 feet with out using a float and no casting is necessary. One thing both of these have in common is that light wire hooks of 3/0 or 4/0 size are best, because these can be straightened out and pulled free when snagged on the bottom or on an old tree stump. Then they can simply be re-bent and put back into their original shape. This saves a lot of time, and it also explains why strong line should be used. Both methods can be used at almost any depth down to about 20 feet according to where you may find the fish. The sinker always holds the line vertical so that no strike can be missed due to slack line if the fisherman has a tight-line. Obviously, that's where the term tight-line came from. So . . . . all you saltwater fishermen that don't have a boat big enough to follow the fish to the oil rigs and the deep water reefs during the cool months, remember, you can still have some fun going Crappie fishing. TIGHT-LINE STYLE!!!!

BASS FISH'N FOR GREEN TROUT

Having been an avid angler for over 40 years and fished in nearly every state, plus parts of Canada and Mexico, I truly believe that the Largemouth Bass or Green Trout (as it is called in the great state of Mississippi) is the most sought after freshwater fish in the North American Continent. Many of today's "big-fish" stories come from Bass anglers who fish the large lakes with sophisticated and expensive equipment. Mississippi's anglers have their share of professional Bass fishermen and they are well aware of the advantages of using such equipment during a big tournament. Massive advertising comes into play when the big name anglers win using big name products. But not much is heard about the everyday weekend fisherman and some of the great catches made on the smaller lakes. In many states, including our own, some of the smallest lakes have produced their share of "HAWGS".

Mississippi has countless small lakes and ponds throughout the entire state that offer excellent Green Trout fishing. Granted, many of these small bodies of water are on private property and only fished if you know the owner. But, there are also many state managed lakes, big and small, that are open to the public for a small park entrance fee. Examples of some popular small lakes are: Mayor Creek, which is only about 700 acres and located about 25 miles east of Laurel. This little lake produces several 10 pounders each year. The Flint Creek Water Park is a favorite for many gulf coast anglers looking for near-by freshwater action. The Pascagoula River has hundreds of small lakes and ponds in and along its tentacle-like waterways located to the north of highway 90 bridge. This mass of bayous, ponds, creeks, lakes and other estuaries produces thousands of Bass annually and never seems to be "fished-out". The Biloxi and Tchoutacabouffa Rivers also have many lakes and ponds throughout the area north of Big Lake and The Back Bay of Biloxi. During the past ten years I have personally caught well over a 1000 Green Trout within 2 miles of the Popps Ferry Bridge. There are some times of the year that you can catch Green Trout and Speckled Trout within a few feet of each other. Pearl river is just a great area to fish. I have also caught Bass and Specks on this river, and on many, many trips have left for home with 'em still bitt'n. Bayous such as Davis, Bernard, Fort, Gravaline, etc., are also very popular Green Trout producers for the local anglers.

Well known large lakes throughout the state are: Ross Barnett Reservoir in Jackson, Okatibbee Reservoir located just north of Meridian, Lake Grenada in Grenada, Enid Lake, located a little farther north off I-55, Sardis Lake, located still further north and just to the east of Sardis, Lake Arkabulia, located about 25 miles south of Memphis, Tenn., Columbus Lake, just north of Columbus, and of course a hot spot in the northeast corner of the state, Lake Pickwick, which also touches the Tenn. and Ala. shores.

Regardless of the size of the water, it must be noted that what may be considered a big Bass in one state or area, may not be in another. However, any fish that is well above the average size for that area is labeled as "Big". I'm sure most Bass anglers will agree that a 5 pound Bass is a respectable catch anywhere but certainly not a trophy fish most places. An 8 pounder is a great catch in most states and a real trophy in some. Now a 12 to 15 pounder gets in to the "HAWG" class and drastically limits the number of states which can routinely produce these lunkers. Why do some areas always produce more and larger fish? There are several factors.

The growth and mature size seems to be directly related to geography, length of growing season, fishing and boating pressure and stabilized fish population, along with a variety of other variables peculiar to any given area. Southern states have longer growing seasons due to warmer temperatures throughout the year. This factor also has a direct effect on food sources and spawning periods. Also contributing to longer periods of activity. Normally, the number of large Bass is small in comparison to the entire Bass population, which automatically increases the odds of catching the "HAWG". But, here again, because of relatively few big Bass taken from most average lakes, anglers tend to underestimate the actual number of lunkers a given body of water may produce. Heavy fishing pressure on a lake may also lead to contradictory thinking, in that many so called "fished-out" lakes can and do produce their share of the wise old "bucket-mouths".

Many frustrated week-end anglers seem to think that to be a successful "Bass-catcher", you need some kind of gimmick or mystical talent along with the expensive and highly sophisticated tackle, specialized techniques and a profound knowledge of the prized and seemingly elusive "HAWG". Actually, what one does need most of all is just a general understanding of the essential elements of the sport. Like, when to fish, where to fish and how to fish. Simple!!

Many anglers say that the best time to fish for Green Trout is anytime . . . . providing it's springtime. Many a Bass is caught in the late summer and fall, but most big time Bass pros say that spring is the best time to catch the heavy-weights. During part of the spring, Bass are spawning or about to spawn and the big females laden with eggs, may be found in shallow water and are fairly accessible to the angler. Also they will weigh more for their length than after spawning and considerably more than the male.

Large plastic worms have historically been the most effective big Bass bait. Some "HAWG" fishermen have even been known to use 12 to 18 inch freshwater eels when fishing for trophy-sized Bass, however, other than in some of our southern states, most North American large mouths never have a chance to even see such a giant meal. Even though most Bass fishermen argue that the best time of year is in the spring, eel and worm baits are very effective during the cooler months, and also when fished deep, in the heat of the summer. Stick baits are another favorite for both the angler and the fish. These dynamic surface lures are the most productive when used by experienced retrievers. No other lure matches the stick bait in ability to bring an angry Bass to the surface in an electrifying strike. Lakes with a lot of stumps, brush and old bottom trash are sure hotspots for stick bait fishing on warm, calm days. Spinners and jigs work well also, but extreme caution must be used to prevent getting hooked on a log, stump or brush. The most effective spinners are those which can be worked the instant they hit the water and continue to work all the way down to and on the bottom. The more one works the spinner bait, the more feel you develop as it bumps into and over snags or other bottom obstructions. The speed on the retrieval must be altered until the right speed produces the best results.

The most realistic of the Green Trout lures are the floating or diving minnow. The old wooden swimming minnow lure is still one of the most productive of its type, and even the newer plastic swimming minnow lures have been productive, including the deep running crank-baits. Realizing that whole books have been written by proven pro-Bass anglers and much is yet to be written on any phase of Bass fishing, I'll conclude with just a few words about some of the local hot spots and how they can be fished. All along the Tchoutacabouffa River, from its mouth to several miles above Cedar Lake, thousands of beautiful Bass are taken annually. Eagle Point, Kates Lake, Four Jacks, Devils Elbow and Cedar Lake are a few of the more well known spots along the river. While Fritz Creek, the Power Plant, the Sisters, Doc's Place and several unnamed hidden inlets north of I-10 bridge seem to be the favorites on the Biloxi River. The Pascagoula Rivers (East and West) offer so many good spots to fish that I could not begin to name even half of them. I will say that I have caught many a Green Trout in the Buzzard Bayous and Moon Lake area off the West river. While the East river has produced fish from Brickyard Bayou all the way up to and including the fork going into Clark Bayou, it is difficult to cover in one days outing. One could spend weeks fishing just sections of the Pascagoula River and still only scratch the surface. And, as with the Pearl River area, I would strongly suggest that you carry a detailed map of the area if you have not fished this great wildlife area. Fort Bayou is a favorite for many. From the bridge in Ocean Springs, to well above the ROA Camp, many a frisky red-eyed Bass has been caught using various lures and techniques. A technique commonly used by the local fishermen, which I briefly mentioned earlier, is using live shrimp or minnows. They may be fished various ways depending upon the time of year, time of day, water temperature, tide and salinity. The smaller Bass seem to always be plentiful along the shallow banks just at the edge of the weed line, either using a small float or just free floating the bait. Working the edge of the drop-offs and mouth of the tributaries are usually productive as the water temperature changes near this area. Some of the larger Bass however, have been caught out in the deep holes away from the banks. During this past fall, I saw only a handful of Green Trout over the 4 pound class. Very few large Bass were taken in the brackish water, however the smaller 1 to 3 pound Bass seemed plentiful. On nearly every trip, my son Steve and I limited out in just a couple of hours. So, as the saltwater species become harder to come by during the few months of our, so called, winter, the Green Trout becomes the primary target for the gulf coast fishermen. You don't have to become a couch potato. Your can get out and participate in one of man's favorite sports. Hit those ponds, lakes, rivers, creeks and any other favorite fish'n hole! And have a good winter and early spring, BASS FISHING FOR GREEN TROUT.

SUNFISH

The young country-boy, Huck-Finn type cane pole fishermen of days gone by and the laid back, sophisticated light tackle angler of today, actually have a lot in common. Most of all, they both obviously enjoy catching the feisty Pan-fish, and the majority like to chow down on the tasty little rascals. But, most of them share a common problem. Most Pan-fish anglers don't know for sure just what they caught sometimes. This is especially true in the case of our various species of the Sunfish family, which abound in our southern freshwater lakes and rivers.

Most of us know what a Bluegill or "Bream" and a Crappie or "White Perch" or "Sackola" look like. Or do we? I have been fishing with folks that fish for Pan-fish on a regular basis that just called them all Bream. That included the Red-Eye Perch, the War-Mouth or Rock Bass or Goggle Eye or any of the other members of the Sunfish family. I have fished in most all of our fifty states plus Canada and Mexico, and even after reading many articles on these little creatures, I still have a hard time identifying some of the various species in the different parts of the nation.

So far, I've found out that if you include the Bass and Crappie, the Sunfish family (scientifically know as centrarchidae) can be divided into two categories based upon the number of hard spines in the anal fin, i.e., those with 3 spines and those with 5 or more. Frankly, I forget to even count when I get to catch'n 'em. But, usually, I can research later and find out exactly what I caught. I don't intend to go through the entire identification and their characteristic markings, but I do think that their various names are interesting and worth knowing. For example, the Sunfish with the 5 or more spines has 7 different species including the 2 Crappies, which should never be confused with any other member of the Sunfish family. Both the black and white Crappie, (pomoxis annularis and pomoxis nigromaculatus) range throughout the entire Mississippi River Basin. The common Rock Bass, (ambloplities rupestris) with its goggle-eyes, is another common Sunfish species all through the Mississippi Valley. As a matter of fact, reports show that the Rock Bass have a natural range from Montana and North Dakota through Onterio and Quebec on south to Tennessee, Georgia, Florida, Alabama, Mississippi, Louisiana, Texas and Oklahoma. Probably the most popular of the Sunfish family fall into the species with 3 anal spines. The Bass, Bluegill, Long Eared Sunfish, Spotted Sunfish, Banded Sunfish, Punkenseed and Red Eared Sunfish, (Shell Cracker or Stumpknocker) all are found in our southern waters. Fishing for these feisty fellows with a, light weight fly rod is about as much fun as any type fishing you can find anywhere. Great sport and great eating.

All of these fish are an integral part of the natural fish chain found in North America, and its members play an important role in the ecological balance of our many freshwater fisheries management. Their value as a big game fish is not always in direct proportion to their size, but as a game fish on light tackle, they rate near the top. Ask any kid with a can of worms and a willow stick or cane pole.

YA GOTTA BE CRAZY

The alarm hadn't sounded yet, as I slipped out of bed and took an optimistic look out the bedroom window. A dozen or so weather forecasters had not been wrong the night before as it was exactly as predicted, a wet and gloomy morning. This didn't dampen my spirits however, for I quickly did my morning normals, dressed and as I finished off a big glass of orange juice, I started to weigh the odds of making it to Chandeleur Island and chase Speckled Trout all day. Go for it!!! I had loaded the car the night before so it was not long before I was cranked up and on my way to meet fishn' partner #1. But even as I backed out of my driveway, with the rain pelting down, I couldn't help but think, "YA GOTTA BE CRAZY". It was a little foggy, and raining pretty hard as I drove into the driveway of the former Outdoor Editor, (the late) John Lambeth. As usual, John was not only ready, but was standing at the door waiting for me with a hot cup of coffee. Since his "Bronco" was already loaded and he had promised to pick up fish'n partner #2, I quickly transferred my gear to his vehicle and off we went. As we cruised along down highway 90, the wind started to pick up a bit, making matters worse, but even then, it was apparent that all of this meant little to any of us as, (the late) Captain Ralph Hyer was ready and waiting when we arrived at his apartment. Seemed in no time at all, we were at the boat slip where the "Silver Nugget" was moored and as we loaded our gear onto the 24 foot Boston Whaler, (the late) Toxey Hall Smith, the 4th member of our elite fishing party arrived. On the way to the boat, the three of us had elected Toxey to be the Captain this trip, by an overwhelming 2 to 1 count. Since the vote was by secret ballot, we didn't know who voted against Toxey, but I'm sure that his owning the boat had a lot to do with him being elected Captain.

It only took a few minutes to stow everything in their neat orderly places and with the approval of our Captain, we cast off the lines and were on our way. The big 275 horsepower Evenrude made it seem like we virtually flew across the water to Biloxi Small Craft Harbor where we picked up fuel and ice from an amused Pat Kuluz. Even (the late) Larry Dubaz took time from reading the morning Sun-Herald to look up and mutter something like, "YA GOTTA BE CRAZY". But, when you put together a former F.B.I. Agent, local attorney, and Coast Guard Auxiliary instructor; along with a former Navy man, pro-bass fisherman and outdoors editor for the Sun-Herald; plus a former tackle shop owner, expert rod builder and licensed 100 ton Captain; and add a old retired fighter pilot, fish story teller and owner of a local bait camp, it would take very bad weather, real angry wives and/or complete engine failure to have stopped us from going at this point. We just smiled and waved good-by as we departed the harbor.

Actually the trip out was not really all that bad, if you don't mind the bumpy road and getting more than a little wet. Boat owner and elected Captain, Toxey Smith, did stop just off of the south side of Ship Island and we re-evaluated the situation. Unanimously we decided to continue on as none of the three reasons to abort mentioned earlier had occurred yet. (very bad weather, real mad wives and/or complete engine failure.) Of course it's only fair to mention that if things had not been totally favorable, Toxey would have overruled all of us, as he is really a very safety-minded skipper and currently a leader in the Coast Guard Auxiliary Rescue program.

As we headed for the "light" which is located on the north end of Chandeleur, Jonn Lambeth stated that if we would go directly to Schooner Harbor he would appreciate it as he wanted to interview, (the late) Rudy Grigar. This sounded great to me as in the excitement of rather we were going to go or not to go, I had forgotten that John also had an assignment for his outdoors section. Besides that, Rudy Grigar was one fisherman that I sure wanted to meet. With the combined efforts of a freshwater Bass fisherman navigating and attorney skipper piloting our great "whaler", we soon had Rudy's houseboat in sight, even with the somewhat limited visibility. But, the rain was still falling as I silently said to myself "YA GOTTA BE CRAZY".

The "Houston Plugger", as he is proudly known in the fishing world, greeted us with a firm handshake and a warm smile as he invited us on board for a, much appreciated, cup of hot coffee. We soon found out that Rudy Grigar was not only an expert fisherman and well qualified guide, but he is also one fine gentleman. The "Plugger" is just about a legend around Chandeleur Island when it comes to Red Fish and Speck fishing. At 71 years young, Rudy has fished, chartered and been a fishing guide around the Chandeleur Island for over 23 years of his 55 years of serious fishing. I could nearly write a book about him after only a short time, and it was easy to understand why outdoors writer, John Lambeth wanted to tell his readers about the "Houston Plugger".

We were enjoying our second cup of coffee as John was deeply involved in his interview, when Rudy appeared to suddenly notice my bright red GCCA cap. He really got excited and stopped the interview to draw our attention to a newspaper clipping tacked to the wall, surrounded by hundreds of great pictures of fish and fishermen. He proudly informed us that in 1977, when he still owned a popular tackle shop in Texas, a group of concerned sport fishermen met in his shop and formed the start of what is now known as the Gulf Coast Conservation Association (GCCA). He was like a teacher telling his students that GCCA is now well over 30,000 members nationwide, including nearly 1,000 in Mississippi. This opened a 30 minute discussion, as it just so happens that John, Ralph, Toxey and yours truly are all members of the local Mississippi Chapter. That Rudy was an early supporter of the association, just further increased our admiration for this legendary fisherman. John still had his portable tape recorder going throughout the whole thing and found himself torn between duty and pleasure when Rudy suddenly stood up and said, "Come on, Let's get ta' fish'n. John, I can still talk to you while we're catch'n fish".

As we stepped outside, it was obvious the temperature was dropping and the wind blown rain hit us in the face as we boarded two of Rudy's large skiffs. "Just right", said our host. "There's fish just wait'n for us and by golly we'll sure gonna catch 'em with the weather like this." We all just kinda looked at each other in somewhat disbelief, but pulled our rain jackets a little tighter and were ready to go. After a short boat ride, we were soon over knee deep wading along the edge of one of his favorite fishing spots. Here again is a story all by itself, and I could go into great detail as to how Rudy positioned everyone and then made the first cast. Well, it was not very long before the Plugger" gave his famous war cry, "Wall to Wall", as he started to work in a nice 5 to 6 pound Red Fish. Almost immediately thereafter, ol' Dick stuck one and before I got mine in, the "Plugger" struck again. This time, a very respectable 3 to 4 pound Speck. Not to be outdone, Ralph let everyone know that he had one on. Then John got into the act with two nice Rat Reds in two quick casts. We fished that spot for another 30 minutes and added four more fish to our stringer as the temperature continued to drop and the wind and rain increased. This was the first time I had ever been wade fishing in less than 3 feet of water with over 4 foot waves hitting me in the chest. Much to our unanimous agreement, Rudy casually suggested that we pick 'em up and head for the "houseboat". We did stop on the way at one of his cultivated oyster beds and picked up a bucket full of some of the most beautiful select singles I have ever seen. It seemed like in no time at all, we were standing on his "fish-cleaning" houseboat, located some 100 yards from his big houseboat. Rudy made oyster shucking and fish cleaning appear to be a quick and simple task as he laid the plump oysters and thick fish fillets out on the cleaning table while we watched in amazement. "Now we can go eat these and have a nice toddy for the body", he quipped to the four cold and hungry fishermen. Once again it was getting close to decision time. The weather was getting worse and the afternoon was slipping away from us. It looked like darkness was even trying to come early. Anyway, we wolfed down nearly a half-gallon of raw oysters while Rudy packed the filleted fish for us to take with us. We all said our goodbye's to Rudy and boarded the "Silver Nugget" for an obvious unpleasant trip home. But, not a grunt could our elected Captain and boat owner get from his 275 horse powered pride and joy. Well, John Lambeth is really a lot more than just an outdoor editor, former Navy man, pro-bass fisherman, loving husband, good friend, etc., he is also a pretty-fair-to-midland outboard mechanic, especially on big Evenrudes, which also happen to be one of his sponsors. So, John starts to trouble-shoot and by the time he finds the problem, we could not help but notice that it had just gotten too late and there was no way that we could make it home before dark now. Plus, we had no idea what the seas were like between the island and mainland. Well, the "Plugger" was sorry that we had a problem, but was openly elated that we had decided to spend the night, and he quickly helped us unload the necessities. The first thing that we did was to notify the authorities and wives. By the time we had notified every one of our intentions, Rudy had the frying pans out and had assumed command of the situation as he barked out requests for his guests to fix themselves a drink and make themselves at home. Wow! We finished off the few remaining raw oysters and by that time our host had fresh fried fish available as fast as we could eat them. All of this Rudy kept referring to as appetizers, as he had been nursing a pot of what he called he seafood 'a le' Chandeleur Special. Needless to say, the four of us were soon four pleasantly stuffed fishermen and we realized that Rudy Grigar was not only a super fishermen, fantastic host, great friend, but also one heck of a cook. Later that evening, we even found out that he was a pretty fair card player as he won most of the toothpicks back that he had so kindly let us use.

Early the next morning, John and Toxey got the "Nugget" started and purr'n like a kitt'n. After enjoying Rudy's great flap-jack, bacon, egg and morning coffee eye-opener, we loaded up, waved goodbye to our new friend and headed out for what proved to be an uneventful trip back to "The World". I'll tell you this, "YA GOTTA BE CRAZY" not to want to go back!!!!

BLUEFISH ARE FUN

Of all the fish caught in the Mississippi Sound, one of the least finicky is the aggressive and hard fighting bluefish. They are known to attack ferociously just about any thing that you happen to drag by their pugnacious nose. That includes live bait, dead bait and all types and sizes of artificial baits. As a matter of fact, the ease in which they can be hooked, make them a favorite among the novice and experienced angler, especially if they are just looking for a little action. Notice I said hooked. I didn't say caught, because a blue is very talented at throwing a hook. Not quite as good as a Lady Fish or a Tarpon, but they can make one look good as a quick catch-and-release artist, especially if using a lure with only one hook.

The sight of a big school of large Blues feeding is one of the most awesome things you will ever see. You can actually see them herd bait fish into a ball and then slash in and out, tearing at their Ray. Sometimes they will even turn clear water into a, rusty white foam from the blood of their kill when into larger baitfish. It's not at all uncommon to see big Bluefish chase schools of bait fish clear up onto the shore with the surf and then come onto the beach themselves while in a feeding frenzy. I remember back in the mid '70s, reading about large schools of big Bluefish chasing baitfish into the shallow swimming beaches around Pompano Beach, Florida, and in their crazed feeding frenzy, slashed the arms and legs of the swimmers. The paper reported that over two-dozen swimmers were taken to the hospital for emergency treatment. The Blue is well equipped with a mouthful of truly impressive razor-sharp teeth. Be aware, they will do their best to bite you when you boat him and as you remove the hook. Do use caution!!

My favorite method to catch these vicious critters is to fish the surf. Many a trip to the surf at Chandeleur Island to fish for Speckled Trout and Red Fish, has been salvaged by a school of Blues, coming along working the sand bars. They swarm through between the sand bars, feeding and attacking about anything that looks like something to eat. For anglers that only keep a few of their fish to eat and just enjoy the thrill of the fight, this type of fishing is really fantastic. I have spent hours, catching and releasing Blues until my arms ached.

I well remember one beautiful early fall morning, my salty friend Grady Cook and I were plugg'n away, catch'n a few, but look'n for a big old Red or Speck to liven things up a bit. Suddenly the water started to boil with feeding activity about a hundred yards up the beach. Within minutes, dozens of seagulls were screeching and dipping down, again and again, snatching bits and pieces, sometimes whole baitfish. Thinking that it was just a school of Hardtails with their normal following of parasites, we went back to fish'n. As the frothing mass began to surround us we recognized several of the toothy feeders and immediately backed up through the foaming surf for the beach. By this time many of the small baitfish had come ashore, apparently preferring suicide on the beach over being caught in the bluefish choppers. As I approached the edge of the beach, I took a hard shot on the side of my leg and jumped the last five feet in the air, thinking that I had been attacked. With one giant step I make the beach in time to see the school feeding right on the edge of the wash. Since we were both still dragging our bait, we both got fish on right away. And having light tackle, we knew we were in for some fun. By this time hundreds of baitfish were Floundering on the beach and along came several of the big Blues right after them. But then the next wave would wash them back into the surf again. My partner beached his fish first and we could not help but admire the sleek, bass-like predator, as it glistened in the sun. Just as Grady was carefully unhooking his fish, my lure came rocketing past me as my fish had thrown the spoon with a terrific jump not more than 10 fee away. By the time I had my second hook-up, Grady was already releasing his second fish. I continued to coax my fish through the surf and with the aid of the next breaker, I successfully dry-docked him on the beach. So far our fish were only in the four to five pound class, however we both had seen Blues much larger breaking in the surf. The real blitz lasted about an hour and as the fish moved on down the beach, we both moved back and sat down with a tired sigh. Neither of us had kept count, but it would not be an overstatement to say that between the two of us we had caught and released close to 50 big Blues. That says nothing about the ones that threw the bait and before we could retrieve it, another had picked it up and made a run. We did land several in the 8 to 10 pound class and really had our hands full, even to just drag them up onto the beach. I did hook one that I would guess to go nearly 14 or 15 pounds, however, with no rodeo going on, we neither one really wanted to keep any of them. As we moved on down the beach in search of Specks or Reds, several more schools of Blues moved by within casting distance, but we were not tempted. We had experienced all the fun we could handle for the day catching Blues. But, I always remember that, "BLUEFISH ARE FUN"!!!!

SHOULD'A STAYED IN BED

It was a dark and cloudy morning, almost 25 years ago, my longtime friend and fishing buddy, the late Grady Cook arrived at my house in his old Pontiac Station Wagon with his trusty 15 foot Blazer boat loaded down with enough tackle for four fishermen and at least a six pack of Dixie Beer. I quickly loaded my tackle and down the road we went. It never mattered whose vehicle we took, Grady always insisted that I be the designated driver. (Remember the Dixie six pick) The game plan was to pick up a couple hundred live shrimp at Popps Ferry Fishing Camp and head west.

We had been looking forward to fishing the Pearl River for weeks, as the "Specks" had been hitting on the Pearl" for some time, but the weather had not been cooperating. But now we were on our way. About 30 minutes down I-10 we noticed patches fog. The closer we got to the turn off on old Highway 90, the foggier it got and by the time we were passing through Perlington, the fog was very thick. When we reached the old, Pearl River bridge, we were down to a crawl just to see to stay on the road. Just as we entered the outer structure of the bridge, the taillights of a vehicle ahead of us came into view and then disappeared. Wow! On a strange bridge, in a heavy fog and now not sure what was ahead. Not a good place to be! Made me think that maybe we SHOULD'A STAYED IN BED!!

Again the lights appeared ahead of us and by the time we crept to within 10 to 15 feet, we saw that it was a truck pulling a boat. Keeping a safe distance while still maintaining visual contact, I slowly followed behind and was not surprised to see, first a left turn signal, and then the brake lights as we came off the other end of the bridge. This is where we were to turn left down to the boat launch. Dead stopped, in the middle of a dense fog and wondering what was our next move, I rolled down my window and unable to see any better, a cold chill ran down my back. I looked at Grady. This was not good. The truck ahead of us then made the left turn, but stopped just as he cleared the highway. So there we set, waiting for him to move on down the road so that we could do the same.

About that time, I heard the familiar sound that a vehicle makes as it crosses the steel grid at the draw on the bridge. There was no mistaking that the on-coming vehicle was moving too fast in this near zero visibility and we were in trouble. I told Grady that I was going to pull over to the right side of the road until the turn off to the launch was clear. But, suddenly, the sound of the closing vehicle was upon us and he locked down his brakes as his headlights came roaring into my rear-view mirror. As fast as I still thought my old fighter pilot reactions were, it all seemed like it was taking forever, as we seemed to move at a snails-pace trying to move off the road. I yelled at Grady to hold on tight, as we were about to be rear-ended. The crunch was deafening and the whole thing was actually over in a second, but sure seemed like it went on and on.

First the loud crash, and the violent contortions that our bodies went through as the truck smashed through our boat and trailer. Glass from the rear window came showering forward on us in a billion tiny pieces. The helpless feeling we had as we were slammed down the road, was suddenly interrupted by Grady's 15 foot, out of control, tri-hull boat came flying over the top of us and bounced off the right front fender before skidding ahead just in front of the car. Even as we skidded to a halt nearly 30 feet down the highway, pieces were still flying by and into the ditches.

Not a word was spoken between Grady and I for several seconds, but I do remember looking at Grady and saying in somewhat of a hysterical voice, that I had always wanted to see a boat that could fly, but this was too much. As we quickly got out of the vehicle to survey the damages, a sudden pang of fear hit me as I saw the position of the totally crippled pick up truck behind us. It was sitting at a 45 degree angle across the West bound lane, with at least four to five feet extended into the East bound lane. The truck had scattered large pieces of wreckage all over the highway. The whole scene spelled disaster. As Grady walked toward his boat to survey his losses, I checked on the driver of the truck and found him walking around his truck in a daze. I then ran across the highway to look for a phone to call for help. Several people had heard the crash and had gathered on the other side of the highway, but just as I was about to ask where the closest phone was, I heard that dreaded sound again and out of the fog at the end of the bridge came another vehicle.

With brakes locked, a truck came screaming to within a few feet of the other crippled truck and then miraculously wheeled around the wreck, only to be confronted with the ditch and numerous road signs. It was obvious that the driver had no control as he side swiped one sign, barely missed another and came within a foot of the boat lying right side up by the ditch. All this scared poor Grady out of another of his nine lives. We all thought that Grady was a goner as the truck actually flew by him with less than a foot of clearance prior to coming to a halt nearly 50 feet on down the ditch. Not knowing what else to do, I just took off running back down the bridge toward the bridge-tenders location as I was sure there would be a phone there. About halfway there, I heard another car approaching the end of the bridge. As the car came roaring out of the fog, I waved frantically and yelled at the top of my lungs. When they saw me they backed off the gas and locked down the brakes as they skidded by. I caught the frantic look on a woman's face as she skidded by and bounced off the right side of the bridge just out of sight. I could now faintly see the lights from the bridge-tenders house and as I came near saw her leaning out of the window. I yelled for her to turn on the bridge caution lights and as I got closer requested that she call the Louisiana State police and the Hancock County Sheriffs' office for immediate assistance. Actually, there were seven vehicles involved by the time the law enforcement officials arrived.

By the time we had picked up the pieces, filled out the accident report, loaded up the station wagon with anything we could salvage it was almost noon. We headed back to the East to Biloxi, to get another boat trailer to pick up what was left of the boat and 25 hp, motor. The vehicle would need some cosmetic work but the old '63 Pontiac got us home with no further problems. There were no fish to show, clean or eat and I could not even talk about the one that got away. But, the "rest of the story" is, Grady Cook and Dick Wilson were up bright and early the next morning and on their way to fish the "Pearl" in my boat, the "Tricky Dick" and this time no fog and never a thought that maybe we "SHOULD'A STAYED IN BED"

SUPER BREAM

Still suffering from late winter "cabin fever"? Tired of being cooped-up day after day and feeling like a couch potato? Looking for some early spring fishing fun? Like to know how and where to catch fish all year long and never even need a boat? Well, let me tell you about a saltwater "SUPER BREAM". I was first introduced to this scrappy and cunning saltwater bait-bandit back in the late 1940's, while visiting on the Gulf Coast with my parents. I had been around water all my life and already and already fished from Canada to Florida Keys. But for some reason I had never gone out to specifically catch this particular fish, and this experience was frustrating. I realized when it was time to head back home that I was no more skilled at catching this elusive and challenging rascal than I was when we first arrived. But, I guess it was a start. Simply described by many veteran saltwater fishermen as "Just and old Sheepshead", this toothy bait-stealer is normally available to saltwater fisherman in the South any time of year, around any old dock or pier and may be caught on even the most primitive fishing gear. They inhabit the Gulf of Mexico waters from the backwater brackish tributaries and bayous, along our coastal shoreline and all the way out to the deep reefs and around the oilrigs off shore. But that's the good news. The bad news is when you actually try to catch them. This black and white striped version of a large fresh water Bream is many times called the "convict fish", and has caused generations of anglers to shake their heads, as one bait after another is removed from their sharp hooks with the skill of a brain surgeon. It is not unusual to lose more than a dozen baits to the same crafty nibbler before hooking him or worse yet, after getting a belly-full, just swimming off. It was years later before I developed the skill to really catch the thief.

Even though I seldom ever fish for this scrappy fighter, I have caught tubs full of them, while fishing for Specks or Red Fish with live shrimp. I personally feel that fishing for Sheepshead is an art practiced by die-hard anglers who totally enjoy landing a fish that can present a challenge to even the most ardent fisherman. Contrary to what many big-time sport fishermen believe, it is a difficult, nerve-wracking task that requires a practiced know-how along with good reflexes and alertness.

Our "SUPER BREAM" can be caught on a variety of baits; however, by far the best bait found is the little fiddler or sand crab. It has a colorful splotch of red and blue on its back and at times it will vary from an almost sandy look to a deep, dark brown. Now here is where the hard work actually begins, as this dandy little bait can run sideways, backwards and forward with equal speed and can hide from view in a split second. Even when fiddlers are most abundant they can be difficult to catch, unless you are very agile and can surprise them away from their holes. The best time to catch them is in the early morning before the sun heats things up. Lots of times you find them hiding under any object that will give them protection and the cooler it is the slower they move. You need at least a couple of hundred of these spider-like looking critters if you expect to catch a cooler full of Sheepshead. Remember, the cooler weather is, the easier they are to catch, but they are more scarce and harder to find because they go deeper into their holes.

As mentioned earlier, another popular bait is live shrimp, but only as a second choice. But, remember that live shrimp are almost impossible to find along the upper Gulf States during the winter months. As a result, the die-hard Sheepshead fishermen, who will claw, scrape or dig to get their favorite bait, may still have to settle for frozen shrimp. But, if you have the touch to catch Sheepshead, you can still catch a bunch even with fresh frozen shrimp. You just have to be a little bit better.

Along the Gulf Coast, there are numerous bridges, jetties, piers, sea walls and shallow water oyster beds that offer good conditions for some great Sheepshead fishing. They seem to school around structures and oyster bed. Once you have some idea as to where they can be found, it helps to know when to fish. The best time to get bites and hopefully fish is during the last half of the outgoing tide and the first half of an incoming tide. Often one can clearly see our "SUPER BREAM" gliding around and around the pilings and other underwater structures, especially during the high tides. Unfortunately they usually don't bite until the tide drops and they can start feeding near the bottom. They do prefer the water to be moving and will often refuse to bite at full high or dead low tide. One proven way to increase your chances of attracting these shrewd fish and possibly encourage a minor to serious feeding frenzy is by chumming. Scattering crushed live oyster or clamshell, even barnacles and any kind of marine crustaceans around the pilings or structures where you are fishing, will usually draw a crowd, if there are any fish in the area. While in this feeding frenzy, they are much more likely to gobble up your bait without their usual cautions and sneak-thief tactics. Lots of times you will not even feel the slightest tug, but will simple see our line move slowly away. That's the time to set the hook! In some cases, you will suddenly be surprised when a hefty Sheepshead just grabs your bait and darts off for the nearest cover. No warning that you can see or feel and seems to out fish me about 2 to 1 every time we go for Sheepshead.

As for the equipment, heavy rods and reels, are a thing of the past unless you are fishing or big winter Black Drum. Heavy gear and clumsy terminal tackle will catch our featured fish more by shear accident, even during a feeding frenzy, then by skill. Most ardent Sheepshead fishermen use a limber rod, seven foot or more, and may even favor a simple can pole, with 15 to 25 pound test line. Even with 20 to 30 pound test line, you can usually still feel the tender bite of the fish and have control over him so as to keep him away from the barnacled pilings. I have found that you get more bites and land more fish if you fish the eddy side of the obstruction on a moving tide. Just lower your line a few inches from the obstruction until you feel the lead touch the bottom. Then reel in a couple of inches off the bottom. Hold the rod with the line between your thumb and finger if using a reeling devise. When using a cane pole, look for any line movement and the slightest nibble. In either case, if you have a real good feel, you'll be conscious of a slight heaviness on the line or pole tip as the fish closes his jaws around your bait without moving or going anywhere. He just simple squeezes the meat off the hook and sucks it in. There are times you may only see the pole dip ever so slightly or your line may move over an inch or two, one direction or another. With a reflex action, set the hook! Many times you will find yourself trigger-happy out of frustration and only imagine that you are getting a bite. But when you do learn to outwit this tricky critter, you'll have lots of fun and the fight of your life trying to get him to the surface without getting your line cut on the pilings. On top of that, if you are fishing from a bridge or high see wall, lifting an angry, flopping and jerking "SUPER BREAM" up to where you are sometimes requires pure luck. Remember, even veteran Sheepshead fishermen come up without bait more often than fish, and they know it didn't just wash off. So, they just re-bait and go back for an instant replay, hoping for better results.

The gluttons convict fish is there, waiting for more and in most cases, sooner or later, he's yours. No Sheepshead takes just one fiddler and swims away. I have cleaned Sheepshead that have had as many as 4 fiddler crabs and the remains of maybe a half dozen shrimp in their stomach and obviously they were still biting when I caught them.

For some the Sheepshead is almost as hard to clean, as it is to catch. However, it does make a gourmet meal that will delight any family at the dinner table. Its white filets are very tasty fried, made into fish paddies or perhaps to simple dress it whole, stuff it with oven bake or crab dressing and bake. I have some Japanese friends that prefer Sheepshead over Red Snapper to make su-shi-me, as they claim the raw Sheepshead meat is better flavored. Personally, even after spending nearly 10 years in the Asian culture, I still prefer mine cooked.

I have observed many a veteran Sheepshead fishermen fill their coolers day after day while fishing from either end of the old Biloxi/Ocean Springs Bridge, but one of the best I have ever seen at catching Sheepshead is a personal friend of mine, named Carzata (Kaiser) Eady. Mr. Eady can be found almost any day of the week during the hours when fishing is at its prime time, just pull'n them in like he knows what he's doing. And he does!! Mr. Eady is regarded by many as one of the most successful Sheepshead fishermen in the area. And I'm a believer. So, if you want to learn a few special tactics and take a lesson or two about how to outwit these crafty bait-stealers, keep your eye on Mr. Eady. He is the greatest at catching "SUPER BREAM"!!!

MAKE MY DAY

Like many other gulf coast anglers, I guess my favorite inshore saltwater fish is the Speckled Trout. To compare a trophy size "Speck" with a big old bucket-mouthed black bass for equal bragg'n rights can start an argument in most coast fishing camps that would be comparable to the famous "Tastes Great" vs. "Less Filling" debate. All will agree, however that both species are majestic and deserving of their highly respected status among sport fishermen. Having pursued both for nearly forty years, I have always quietly promised myself that if I ever landed a ten pounder of either species, the taxidermist would be the first to know. Well, after spending untold hours and unaccountable dollars, I am still looking for, my first ten pounder. I must confess, however, that I did catch a Speck that I just had to have mounted. No, it wasn't a ten pounder and it wasn't even the largest Speck that I had ever caught, but it was and still is one of the most beautiful of its species I have ever seen, alive or mounted. Its lines and color were truly magnificent and even now, it looks as if it could swim right off the front of my fireplace. I remember well that day, late last summer, when as usual, I was out looking for that fish that would "MAKE MY DAY".

It was still dark as I parked in front of Wilson's Fishing Camp down on "Point Caddie" in Biloxi, Mississippi. My good friend and fish'n buddy, Mike Chester, greeted me at the door with a cup of hot coffee and with that familiar twinkle in his eye asked, "Where to s'morning, Bo?" I was not surprised that Mike was there waiting on me as he is always ready to go fishing, day or night, except during hunting season, which was by the way, just around the corner. As we loaded up with snacks, cold drinks, live shrimp and a couple of bags of fresh squid and shrimp, we decided where we were going and what we would fish for first.

Since the water was nice and smooth "out front", we headed for the outer rock pile, just inside Ship Island. Eager to wet a line, it seemed like it took forever to get to the barrier island hot spot. As expected, the water was dead slick as I gently lowered the anchor just on the West end of the rock pile. As the anchor rope drew tight on the cleat and the boat moved slightly to line up, I noticed a trace of current movement behind the boat. The tide was just starting to rise. By the time I got baited and in the water, Mike had already landed a real nice White Trout and was going back after another. Fishing the bottom with just a slip-shot for weight, Mike quickly set the hook and landed another nice White Trout, while jerking and popping of my cork, produced nothing. By the time Mike had put his third nice White Trout in the box, I was about convinced that I should give up on catching a Speckled Trout, and should just fish the bottom for White Trout. But just then my cork disappeared. Caught by surprise and completely unprepared, I missed the fish as I tried to set the hook and that didn't make me too happy! Especially when my ardent fishing buddy was just taking off his fourth fish to my zero. To add insult to injury, he then added a small Speck before I could re-bait and get back into the water. On the verge of complete frustration, as my angler's pride made my face burn, I picked out the biggest and most active live shrimp I could find and vigorously cast to the far side of the rock pile. Suddenly I was in business. This time Mr. Speck committed suicide. In shorter time then is normally very smart, I put my first fish into the cooler. A nice two and a half, to three pound Speck. Great!! The black cloud had lifted! The morning sun was shining bright! From then on it was catch-up, put on a cork and join in the fun. And, that's exactly what Mike did. Mike's Ma-Ma didn't raise no fool when it came to fishing. Mike knew that he could come back to the White Trout, but you got to go for the Specks when they are there.

Our fun was short-lived however, as we had only caught about three more fish each when both of our lines were cut by some sharp-toothed fast-mover. Just hit, run and was gone, with my hook still in his mouth. Not knowing for sure what the culprits were, but knowing that mono-line was not the answer, we switched to steel leaders, re-baited and got with it! It didn't take too long, nor were we surprised when we both got hits almost simultaneously and quickly landed a couple of small, but scrappy Blacktip Sharks. Apparently a school of these leathery-skinned scavengers had invaded the area and quickly interrupted our Speck, feeding spree. Actually, it was kinda fun, as we did have our hands full for the next half-hour or so. When we did hook a brave Trout out on the edge of the area that we were fishing, we seldom got the whole fish back to the boat as our new "rulers of the rock pile" usually took their share. Then, all of a sudden, they were gone. None. Zero. Nothing. We couldn't even get an old, hard-head Catfish to bite. We fished the rock pile for about another ten or fifteen minutes in hopes that things would pick up again, but no soap. Nothing even touched our beautiful live shrimp. Not even a crab. It was like every fish within a mile radius of us suddenly got lockjaw. So, we reeled in and were happy now that we had kept three of the larger Blacktip Sharks and they looked pretty good in our cooler along with the twenty or so Specks and White Trout we had. Oh yes, I forgot, we also had a nice fat Ground Mullet that Mike caught just before switching over to the cork. Normally, this would not be a bad catch for the two of us, however, we had both promised friends that we would bring them some fresh fish, so we really needed to get with it or lose our self respect and image. Up came the anchor and away we went to the next hot spot.

As it was, we didn't move very far. Just to the East of the rock pile where there were patches of grass in about 6 to 8 feet of water and at times produced some great Trout. But, this was not one of those times, as we drifted slowly over dozens of dark grassy spots while working our live shrimp. After nearly an hour, we only had two Specks big enough to keep, so we headed on to the next spot. This time it was the "Fort" on the West end of Ship Island. By noon, we still had not gotten into them again, so we headed in to the mainland. Normally there are plenty of White Trout and Ground Mullet on the oyster reefs located just offshore. The tide had started to move pretty good by the time we anchored over the "white house reef" and things really looked right, however it took about 15 to 20 minutes to locate the fish and get them to start feeding. Once they started, however, we caught plenty and we left them still biting, as we had enough by then for us, and our friends too.

Well, just like when you been out bass fishing, and your head'n back to the house, it's really hard to pass up a spot where you have always caught nice fish, and that day was no exception. As we headed up the channel between Biloxi and Deer Island, I stopped twice to check out a couple of favorite hotspots, but didn't even get a nibble either place, so on to the dock. As we were passing the old sunken boat on the sand bar across from the Factory Restaurant, I had a sudden impulse to try one more place. Commonly known as the "Island Reef", the old boat has on occasion produced some pretty fair fish. As we lowered the anchor at just the right spot to fish the swirling tide at the stern of the old boat, I could swear that I smelled fish feeding. There were a few birds working near the boat and every so often I saw a swirl or the flip of a tail. Never could quite make out what was causing it, and even though Mike thought for sure that it was just Popeye Mullet, I hoped he was wrong. Our first two casts produced nothing, even as the tide carried our corks in perfect formation past the stern of the boat. The next time my cork seemed to slow down and made a little bob much like the bait was dragg'n bottom. But, when I brought it in to cast again, my bait was gone. My instincts told me it was a fish, but my skeptic, better judgment, said the bait, no doubt got rubbed off by the sharp oyster shells on the bottom. One more time, I thought, as I carefully selected the biggest of the few remaining shrimp we had left, and skillfully placed my cork within an inch of the stern of the boat. Just as the cork was about to clear the boat, it leaned over a bit just before it gradually disappeared. I gently took up the slack line and as the line tightened, I vigorously set the hook. At first, I thought that I was hung up on the bottom and then I felt a solid shake and I thought maybe I had hooked into a Sting-Ray or, better still, a big old fat Flounder. But that thought didn't last long as my line started moving away from the boat with a strong, steady pull. As the tension increased and the pole bent into a nice "C" shape, I felt several quick, hard jerks on the line, much like a frisky Rat-Red, or even a good, sized Speck. The more I fought the fish with my stiff little graphite rod, the more I worried about rather I was going to land this baby, as sometimes he would bend the rod nearly double, while taking out 20 to 30 feet of line. Plus, I was concerned that at any minute, he would turn around and run back for the boat; where he could easily cut my 12 pound test line. By this time I was fairly certain that I had hooked a nice 4 to 5 pound rat-red, as his runs were strong and heavy feeling. Finally, when I got him to within about 20 feet of the boat, he broke the surface of the water and I was elated to see a beautiful, big Speck. At that very minute, he looked to be at least 10 pounds or more, and I suddenly became very cautious. When he finally gave up and rolled over on his side, Mike was right there ready with the net. He leaned over and made a nice smooth scoop and would you believe it? The darn thing made, one last ditch effort to escape and flopped across the edge of the net, taking drag as he darted under the boat. Boy, howdy, was I glad my Daddy always told me not to be changing my drag too much, even when you got him whipped. This baby would have snapped my line for sure if I would've had my drag too tight. Well, my heart still skipped about ten beats as I plunged the rod tip deep into the water to keep him from cutting my line on the bottom of the boat. Fortunately, he was hooked good and very tired from his hard battle and I had little difficulty bringing him back to the side of the boat for Mike to make a second and successful try. Once into the boat, I realized that this was not my long sought-after 10 pounder, but I was immediately impressed with it's color and strong lines. This was by far, the best looking old yellow-mouthed Speckled Trout that I had seen for quite a while. I was still feeling that little tremor of excitement, from the thrill of the battle, as I re-baited my hook and cast back by the stern of the boat.

We worked our bait all around the stern and sides of the old boat for another 10 minutes with negative results, so up came the anchor and once again we headed for home. Now that really topped things off, and I hope I never get over the excitement of catching a big fish. I didn't even mind cleaning fish for an hour or so when we got back to the fishing camp. As I looked at my catch-of-the-day, which seemed to stretch the entire length of my 64 Qt. cooler, I decided right then and there that it was just too pretty a fish to clean and eat.

Well, you know the rest of the story. My Speck is now in a place of honor on Dick Wilson's fireplace, along side of a 46 pound Bull Red I caught in the early 70's and didn't realize that it was a state record until I had it mounted and, of course, by then it was too late. But, that's another story. So, remember, keep a tight line, take a kid fish'n and you too will say, "MAKE MY DAY!"

YOU AIN'T GONNA BELIEVE IT,
BUT IT'S TRUE

No, this is not just another fish story about the "one that got away", or about how one of my fishing buddies and I just about got killed, or even about one of the most productive fishing trips that I have ever been on. It is however, a story about a week of fishing that I will never forget.

About 20 years ago, one of my favorite lifetime fishing buddies, who by the way, is also my eldest son, Steve, graduated from a highly sophisticated and competitive NAVY electronic data school. He was also promoted to E-4 after only 12 months of active duty upon graduation. Being an old military retiree, I felt I needed to see this graduation, even if it was Navy. So, Steve's mother, (Jacky) and I started saving all our pennies, robbed all the piggy banks, stopped paying all the bills and still flew "space A" to California for this proud event.

I guess my story actually starts shortly after we landed at the San Francisco International Airport, because from that time on, graduation and promotion seemed to take a back seat to man's "second" favorite sport. Steve was there to meet us and really looked great. After a year of hard study it looked like Navy life was agreeing with him. As we traveled the busy interstate to Vallejo, where his quarters were located just outside the gate to Mare Island, the only thing he talked about was fishing. Needless to say, his mother's attempts to tell him all about the family back home, fell upon deaf ears. To hear him talk, you would think that the Navy had sent him out there on a fishing expedition instead of to attend a tough electronics school. By the time we reached his two story duplex, he had completely outlined the whole week, right up to the time we were to get on the airplane and head back to Biloxi.

Within minutes after arriving at his quarters, I had changed my clothes and we were on our way to pick up bait so we could go fishing the rest of the day. The bait consisted of live grass shrimp, which were sold by the pound and really seemed quite small when you're used to fishing with Gulf of Mexico shrimp.

Plus, there were various types of bottom dwelling minnows, some resembled our bull minnows, while others were like nothing I had ever seen before. We arrived at one of Steve's favorite fishing piers well before dark and the tide was just starting to fall. The pier was located on Mare Island Naval Station, near the mouth of the Napa River, which empties into the San Pablo Bay along with the great Sacramento River. Here, Steve informed me, the tide makes a 3 to 5 foot change, so we were there at the right time and should be in for some good fishing. He advised that the experienced anglers out there also fished the tide.

As we rigged and baited, Steve appeared to be upset about forgetting his can of WD-40, however, since we were only going to fish a few hours, and he had brought along a couple of extra rods and reels, I really didn't see any need for alarm. But he was still cussing himself as he made his first cast. Within an hour the tide was moving out at a very noticeable rate and the last rays of the sun were becoming history. Fishing was a little slow; I mean real slow, like nothing, after an hour of staring the rod tips hoping something would make them move. But, it did give father and son a chance to catch up on all that had happened in our lives during the past year. Plus, he briefed me on the various methods and techniques he had learned out there that were different from what we use fishing the Gulf of Mexico and the waters in the Mississippi Sound.

Shortly after dark, some fairly nice sized fish started slapping the top of the water, just inside the shadow of the pier. "Stripers"! Steve yelled, as he grabbed one of the lightweight rods and motioned for me to do the same and follow him to the other side of the pier near where all the noise was coming from. Careful not to let our shadows to show on the water, we cast parallel to the pier, just to the edge of the shadows. On the first cast we were both rewarded with a sharp strike that bent our light graphite rods nearly double. As the white flurry of action neared the pier, Steve landed the fish and released it as gently and quickly as possible. Thinking that mine was a little bigger, I played it longer, only to find out that it was also too small. We managed to entice a dozen or so Stripers to go for the artificial, however, none of them qualified as "keeper" size for that state, so they were also quickly released with no harm other than a sore mouth. Also during the course of the evening, we "think" we might have missed a couple of "hits" on the big rods. But, since this is not the real meat of my story, let me conclude the happenings of that evening by simply stating that we headed for "da house" at about 9 p.m. without a "keeper", however, the companionship we shared will be kept forever.

The next morning, we were up and dressed shortly after dawn, as this was graduation day and things were to get off to an early start. The ceremony was very nice and quite short, making it possible for us to go by special services, rent a boat and motor, hurry home, change clothes and be on the water shortly after 10 a.m.! Now that's what I call a short ceremony and gett'n things moving. This time we were going after Sturgeon. And, this time, I could not help but notice that Steve made a special point not to forget his deluxe size can of WD-40. As we motored around the southern end of Mare Island, Steve rigged the heavy rods with 60 pound test braided wire leaders about four feet long, with a bright new 6/0 stainless steel hook, while I was checking our bait to make sure that it was all still alive and healthy. I gently lowered the anchor about a half-mile off the Southeast corner of the island, just on the edge of a good looking tide-rip and now it was time to get ready to do some serious fish'n. After loading up my hook with a couple of the largest of the grass shrimp, I noticed that Steve was "lubricating" his bait. By that I mean, he was spraying his shrimp with WD-40!! I could not believe it!! What in the world was he doing? Was I seeing things? Where in the world have I been? I laughed and made a joke of it by asking if he thought that it would help make his bait slip though the water easier. He just smiled and offered me the can of WD-40. Being a born skeptic when it comes to fish tales, I shook off his offer and returned his smile as I made a neat cast right into the middle of a large slick that looked too promising to miss. No sooner did my bait hit the bottom than the tip of my rod began to bob and my heart did a flip. I just knew that I had a bite already, and I got ready to set the hook. I stole a glance at Steve to see if he was looking at me and noticed that his rod tip was doing the same thing as mine. What bothered me was that he was acting like he never even notice. When I asked him about it, he advised that it was just the strong tide moving against the line and that he would tell me when I got a bite. Imagine, he would tell me when I got a bite!!! As I sat there thinking about what would be the best way to handle his impertinence, Steve sat straight up, pointed to his rod tip and said, "Now that's a bite!" Sure enough, his rod, bent down slowly and then back up again. Just as it was starting to bend down again, Steve set the hook with a powerful upward swing of the rod. For a brief moment, it looked like he was hooked on the bottom, for the heavy rod bent nearly double as he applied near maximum pressure to the 60 pound test line. But, then the rod seemed to give a quick shake and the fight was on. Sometimes he pumped and gained a little bit of line, much like you have to do when you have hooked into a big Sting Ray. The next minute he would reel in line like there was nothing on the other end. After about 20 minutes of this give and take, the take started taking and the giving became rare. Soon a long dark shape appeared just below the surface about 10 feet out from the boat. "Good, it's a nice size Sturgeon," Steve exclaimed. "Get ready, Pop. You'll have to use that little gaff-hook when he gets tired enough that I can get him up to the boat", he advised between puffs of labored breath. Looking around for a gaff, I finally spotted the "gaff-hook" in the bottom of the boat. It was nothing more than an extra large weighted treble hook, tied to a 10 foot long piece of quarter-inch rope. After what seemed like forever, the big Sturgeon finally rolled to the surface, "plum tuckered out", and Steve skillfully lead it alongside the boat to my waiting gaff. At what I thought to be the appropriate time, I stuck the large treble hook into the oval mouth of the prehistoric looking creature, and with an accompanying karate yell, stood up and jerked the heavy fish over the gunnel and into the boat. Just as it hit the bottom of the boat, the tired and lifeless form suddenly became re-energized, and started beating the heck out of the boat. But, fortunately, before it could do any damage, Steve quickly gave it a hard love-tap on its head with his lead-weighted fish equalizer. Since it was only a stunning blow, we hurried and put in on a heavy nylon stringer and slipped it overboard. By the time we got the end of the stringer secured to the back of the boat, Mr. Sturgeon was starting to come around and was not too happy with being all strung up. But, outside the boat was the best place to keep fish like him. Large Sturgeon has been known to literally tear up a boat before they could be subdued.

Well, since my bait had not been touched, I cast right back into the rip, hoping to catch one before Steve could get back in the water again. I really needn't have hurried, as Steve was methodically re-baiting his hook and made a point to show me that he was giving it a good shot of WD-40 before he threw back in. During the next 30 minutes, Steve caught two more, smaller Sturgeons and released them unharmed. What really bothered me, however, was the fact that he had also missed a couple of other bites while I had not even gotten so much as a bump. Finally, I got the message, loud and clear. After putting on a nice fresh shrimp, I sheepishly asked Steve if I could see his can of WD-40 for a "sec". Not wanting to let me off too easy, he rolled his eyes at me and said, "Gee, Pop, is something wrong with your reel"? As my "lubricated" bait hit the water and disappeared beneath the surface, a tell-tell "oil" slick moved on with the tide. Much to my great joy, within minutes, my rod tip began to quiver and bounce about, much like when a Sheepshead is nipping at your bait. True to his promise, but much to my aggravation, Steve advised me that I now had a bite. As I felt a heavy tug on the line, I set the hook and was disappointed not to find a heavy resistance at the other end. As luck would have it, my first catch of the day was not an elusive Striper, but was a small Striper, referred to by many as a "Shaker". (Too little to keep, so they just hold them out over the water and shake them off.) Well, this time when I baited up, I was not the least bit too proud as just sprayed a generous amount of WD-40 prior to casting back into the rip. I guess I have led a rather sheltered life during my 50 plus years of fishing. I have been preached to since I was big enough to sit in the bottom of a boat, that you do better without man-made smell, such as aftershave lotions, insect repellent, gasoline, oil or any petroleum by-products. And now here I am, intentionally spraying a lubricant directly on my bait. I mean, on purpose!! Before the day was over, we caught several more Sturgeons, however none were over the legal keeper size of 40 inches, so they were released. We also caught a few more little "Shakers" and released them too. And, that's the way the whole week went. I must admit that I did hold out each day and try to catch a fish without using WD-40, however each time I got "out-fished". Each time I found out, "No WD-40, no keeper fish." By the time I had to leave the beautiful tributaries that flow into the San Pablo Bay, I was convinced that WD-40 was the name of the game out there and as I told you all at the very start of this story, "YOU AIN'T GONNA BELIEVE IT, BUT IT'S TRUE!!"

THE ONE'S THAT GOT AWAY

During the past 40 years, I have had the opportunity to go fishing in every state in our great nation, including Alaska and Hawaii, plus some real neat, productive waters in Canada, Mexico, a couple of countries in Europe and a number of countries in the Far East and Asia. I grew up near a chain of beautiful fresh water lakes in northern Indiana and caught my first 5 pound bass well over 50 years ago, at the ripe old age of nine. My father and uncle started me fishing early and by the time I was 12. I truly knew the thrill of playing a hard fighting fish on light tackle and the anguish of losing one right at the very end of the battle. One would think that the thrill, excitement and challenge of hooking and landing a lunker or a deep sea monster would diminish as the years go by, but it ain't so! Nor is it true that things become so routine you don't care, or that maybe I shake less or feel any better when I lose a good fish, than I did years ago. But, one thing is true. Most of the times that I lost a fish, it was my own fault, and that, my friends has not changed. I'm confident that I don't lose as many as I used to, however, I still can tell stories about THE ONE'S THAT GOT AWAY.

Actually, there are many reasons why we lose fish and there are many ways of increasing our odds and percentages to land more fish. Some of the most common reasons that fish get away are: We get into a hurry and don't play the fish correctly. We didn't have the drag set properly prior to the strike or did not adjust the drag at the right time or maybe made the wrong adjustment when we really didn't need any adjustment or using a dull hook or the improper size hook for the type fish caught. Forget about the old line on the reel and that it was half rotten, and we hurried a "green fish" before it was worn down. And of course, there are combinations and a "zillion" other reasons, all of which are usually realized much too late . . . . The big one got away.

You would think that with all of those years of experience, of reading and actually doing the do's and don'ts, one should be able to catch and land every fish hooked. Not true. But, a few basic steps or precautions that you can take to increase your odds are; first, of course, you have to hook the fish. Sometimes you may have to even think like a fish to get him to bite. Now, that doesn't sound like too much of an intellectual challenge to those who are not really into fishing, but to the experienced anglers, they know there is something to this. After years of playing "hide-and-seek" and "hey dar fish, looky what I got for you", one learns to respect the cunning instincts of the wise old trophy size fish. Of course, the fish do have a couple of known advantages. They know the territory much better than you and usually can move about with out you seeing them. On the other hand, an experienced angler is supposed to know where they lurk, what they should be feeding on at that time of year, in what body of water and the proper technique to entice a hook up. Once you get by all that and are making frequent hook ups, but still losing fish, something is not right! There are several possible reasons to be sure, however providing you have played the fish correctly and you equipment is compatible for the size of the fish you have hooked, there are only a couple of fairly common reasons for losing a fish. Pure and simple, probably poor drag control and plain old dull hooks. I'm sure, that many have either read or heard my friend Captain Ralph Hyer go into great detail regarding hook selection and keeping a good sharp hook. A strong believer that the most common mistake made by even some seasoned anglers, is to fish with hooks that are not sharp enough to penetrate the fish's mouth. And he is absolutely correct!! I mentioned earlier that you have to sometimes think like a fish. Well, you also need to know something about the physical structure of these finny creatures too. One needs to understand that the fish's mouth must have an unbelievable resistance to punctures and penetrations by sharp objects, or otherwise, some of its natural food would tear gaping holes all around their mouth. A feisty crab or crawfish or even some of the more spiny bait fish are not going to be eaten without a fight, however, seldom to we see a fish's mouth injured from it's natural food source. The hard bone out-line of the fish's mouth is nearly impossible to penetrate, and almost never by a dull hook. Experienced tarpon and bonefish anglers will tell you in a heart-beat that even with sharp hooks, many fish are lost, however, it a fact that most fish are lost with a dull hook. Even with a good, powerful and pole-bending strike, setting the hook on the initial run with great force, the hook can still start to come lose and work it's way free, all because of a dull hook. However, a real sharp hook will many times re-hook its self again. Sometimes, this can occur several times before the fish is landed. A dull hook often will slide along the inside of the mouth and fail to catch hold again until just at the edge of the mouth where the hard bone makes it near impossible to make penetration. Many fish are lost simply because the hook was not sharp enough to make good, deep penetration on the initial hook up. A simple test to check the point of any hook is to place the point against your thumbnail and drag it across under slight pressure. If the point doesn't dig in immediately, the hook need sharpening or replaced.

There are many ways and means to sharpen a hook, but any type of sharpening is an improvement. There are several tools or devices for sharpening hooks, some better than others, however, all of this is an article of it's own. The important thing here is to be aware and get in the habit of checking your hook each and every time that you go fishing. Another area of extreme importance and often overlooked sometimes even by experienced anglers, is drag control. Here again, there are a lot of variables to keep in mind. A common mistake is not testing your drag prior to the first cast, especially if you have not been fishing recently. Saltwater fishermen have to always be on the alert for corrosion, which may prevent the reel from operation properly and before you know it, you've lost your fish. Some other important factors to remember when setting the drag is line strength, rod and reel compatibility, type and size fish you are fishing for and type bottom or habitat you are fishing over. Even ones individual experience and knowledge of fishing for a specific fish in a specific location enters into the overall picture. There are actually only a few ways to judge how much or how little drag to set, as each rod and reel has a different feel. The primary factor is usually individual experience and preference. I've fished with some real "Salties" that prefer to keep a relatively lose drag and even after the initial strike, will continue to let the fish run, long after most anglers would have set the hook. Long time veteran angler and personal friend, (the late) Grady Cook, will let a fish run and run and finally, when it's ready to bring to the boat, he will gradually tighten down the drag. Lots of patience. But, I'm here to tell you, Grady just doesn't miss many fish, so it must be a good technique for him. Sometimes a fish will feel the pressure and drop the bait before you can set the hook. Or there may be some nearby underwater obstructions to cut the line, so it does depend a lot on what you're fishing for and where your fishing. I have also seen other anglers that want immediate control, and keep their drag so tight that they have broken their line just setting the hook on a big fish. Other times they have had the line break from forcing a green fish too quickly and lost the fish right next to the boat. Most Bass fishermen have learned proper drag technique early. Good Bass fishermen like my friends Jim Randolph from Long Beach and John Lambeth of Biloxi, seldom lose a fish out in open water and are amazing in heavy brush, adjusting the drag as necessary to keep the fish clear while still not over challenging the line. I have learned to change my drag as the situation dictates, but usually you can find that happy medium for most fish. Here again, experience seems to be the predominant factor and on the first run, you know about how close you are to the best setting. I have seen times when I've brought a big fish right up to the boat in a relatively short time without ever touching the initial drag setting, only to have the fish flip water in my face and rip off another 50 feet or more of line in a last ditch effort as he saw the boat. Needless to say, had I been in a big hurry to land him and tightened down on my drag as he appeared to tire next to the boat, he could have easily snapped the line. No one can really teach you all the best techniques and tell you all the "do's and don'ts" regarding any part of fishing. Like everything else in life, experience is the key factor, however, it sure doesn't hurt to watch and listen. Fishing is truly a sport of luck, skill and practice. Believe me when I say that you need it all plus a silent prayer sometimes to keep from having to talk about THE ONE'S THAT GOT AWAY.

A DAY TO REMEMBER

The cool gray dawn, in year 1991, was just beginning to show signs of being interrupted by the first faint glow of the early morning sun. A slight breeze rustled through the tall pines that surrounded the marina's shoreline and seemed to whisper, "It's gonna be a great day". Our pace gradually quickened as we methodically loaded the 20 foot Critchfield, placing everything in its rightful place. It was Saturday and time to go fish catch'n!! The past week had seemed exceptionally long and I was really looking forward to the weekend, especially since my sister, Juanita, and her late husband, Gordon had just arrived from Huntington, Indiana on Friday. Gordon and I had immediately made plans to take my lively 10 year old twin boys, Mike and Marty, fishing. (Who by the way are 49 years old now) Like we needed an excuse to go! Loaded down with more tackle than we could possibly use in a week, an abundance of fresh and frozen bait, snacks, cold drinks, beer, sun tan lotion, large and small ice chests and even rain gear for everyone, I began to wonder if we had enough power to get the boat up on to a plane. As we edged over to the fuel pumps, I told Gordon to have the attendant top off the saddle tanks while I went to the office to pay for the gas and pick up ice. Upon return to the boat, I checked the security of all the fuel caps and prior to firing up the engine, I went through my normal, self-imposed check-list. After nearly 20 years of flying fighters, it's difficult to even start my car without doing some kind of preflight check . . . . or something.

Everyone was informed where the life preservers were, the C.B. radio was checked, engine cover cracked open and the engine compartment exhaust blower was on. I instructed the twins to always move forward away from the engine area whenever I was starting the engine as I have seen far too many gasoline engines blow up during starting. With the mandatory anti-spark resister, it is not supposed to happen, however I know of too many cases where it didn't work that way. As I opened the engine compartment cover, I thought I detected a faint smell of gasoline, but having just refueled and not seeing any visible signs of fuel in the bilge, I went ahead and cranked the engine. The powerful marine engine quickly came to life and in a matter of minutes we were clear of the marina and skimming across the calm waters of the Biloxi Back Bay. Destination . . . . Ship Island and it's famous Camille Cut, located just 9 miles off the coast in the beautiful Mississippi Sound. In less than 30 minutes from the time we left the Keesler Marina, I cut back the throttle and while Gordon steered the Critchfield toward the mouth of the cut, I quickly rigged and set out four trolling lines at intermittent depths and staggered lengths behind the boat. Satisfied that they would not tangle in the turns, I returned to the controls and was about to announce that I saw a school of Spanish Mackerel ahead, when one of my rods began to buck and bend as the line on the deep sea reel was giving up over a hundred feet of line in a few seconds. As I reduced power a little, I yelled at Gordon to grab the rod in hopes that he would draw first blood. Just as he started to head the first catch of the day toward the boat, that familiar drag alarm sounded again, this time from the other corner of the stern. I cut the power back some more and quickly moved toward the other bent rod. As I started to retrieve the fish, I realized that it was not a real big fish, so I handed the rod to the closest twin, which just happened to be setting right next to the rod holder. His big smile was worth a thousand words as he leaned into the task like it was a 2000 pound Marlin. Back at the controls, I picked up the speed just a wee bit to ensure we maintained good tight lines on the fish and was about to give some of my expert advise when all at once the third reel started screaming as the line tore off at an alarming rate. Once again I slowed down some to check it out, but this time the line went slack as I picked up the rod from the holder. What ever was there a second ago was there no more, so I handed the rod to the other twin and told him to crank it in, check the bait and that he got to catch the next fish. By this time Gordon had his fish fairly near and it appeared to be out running the boat. I advanced the throttle a little and the fight was resumed. It looked like it might be a Jack-Crevalle, the way it seemed to hang out to the side. Even though it was not taking out any more line, it was still all Gordon could do to hold what he had. I patted Gordon on the back and with tongue-in-cheek, told him to, "Keep his head up", and went to see how Mike was doing with the other fish which he had almost to the side of the boat. As I grabbed the 60 pound leader, I told Marty to open the ice chest and I would swing our first keeper of the day into the box. With one fluid motion, I swung the nice 2 pound Spanish Mackerel into the ice chest and pinned its head between the lid and the chest like a vice, while I quickly removed the hook. About that time, Gordon let us know that he was ready for some help to get his fish on board, so I picked up the long handled gaff and as the nearly 30 pound beauty rolled onto his side, I gently stuck the point of the gaff into the lower lip and with one swift movement lifted the Jack's head up just high enough to remove the hook. As I gently released the tired but unharmed fighter, Gordon gave me that look of panic and ask me what I was doing. After all that work, why throw back a perfectly good fish? I moved the throttles forward again and headed back to the area that we had caught the fish and explained to him that the Jack-Crevalle was an excellent sport fish to catch, but not very good to eat. Therefore, most anglers released them to fight again another day.

We continued to troll back and forth, in and out of Camille Cut with above average success. Sometimes we had fish on all four lines at the same time. By noon we had over 40 nice Spanish Mackerel, two Red Fish in the 30 pound class and had two lures cut off by large fish, which were probably Shark from the way the line was frayed. Hoping to get into a school of Red Fish, or maybe even a nice big Lemon Fish, (Cobia) we ventured out along the south side of Ship Island. However, it was not too long before the wind came up and the seas began to get rough, forcing us back behind the island. I had seen what 20 to 25 knot winds could do to a small boat in open water, so I figured we would just troll around inside for a while until either the winds changed or we were force to head for the mainland.

Since it was only mid-afternoon, and basically a beautiful day, I decided to stop by an old sunken barge that was located just to the east of the Ocean Springs Ship Channel along about marker #8. It didn't take us long and we were soon anchored over the wreck and pulling in White Trout, Croaker and Sheepshead with just about every cast. However, this great fun was short lived as within 30 minutes the seas built up 3 to 5 feet, even behind the island. Reluctantly, I announced that the time had come to head for the house. Amid the moans and groans from Mike and Marty, we stored the gear and got the boat ship-shape for the trip home. The normal procedures were accomplished including the engine compartment cracked, blower on and all crew members forward. Gordon automatically moved to the bow ready to retrieve the anchor as soon as I cranked the engine. I turned the key and immediately heard that dull, click-like sound that only one whom has heard it before, can readily identify it. A sound that is usually, immediately followed by a crackling explosion caused by the igniting of fuel fumes. That's right, the engine blew up, sending flames out in all directions and the entire aft section of the boat was instantly on fire. As I grabbed the twins, I noticed that the back of Marty's shirt was on fire, which I quickly beat out with a boat pillow. Fortunately, he had worn an old sweatshirt over the top of his tee shirt and never got burnt. The life jackets were within reach under the bow, so I threw Gordon one, picked up Mike and set him on the bow and as I reached for another life preserver, Marty practically flew over the windshield on to the bow with Mike and Gordon. I gave each a life jacket and told them to put them on and hit the water. Without hesitation, Gordon, and the twins slipped into the jackets and were over the side in a few seconds. By this time, the heat from the fire drew my attention to the back of the boat and to my amazement, the flames were literally licking at my feet. A feeling of helplessness and frustration washed over me as I witnessed the boat and all of our tackle being totally consumed by flames. As I reached for the remaining life jacket, flames were suddenly all around me and I heard Gordon's voice above the roar of the fire yelling, "Come on! Get the hell out of there!" As if suddenly broken from a trance, a shot of adrenalin pumped through my system and I must have cleared well over six feet as I leaped from the burning boat. Since I had no life preserver, I quickly swam to the others. We all got close together and I was supported by their combined flotation. Thankfully, with the aid of the wind and tide, we were soon carried well away from the scorching flame and the danger of the remaining fuel tanks exploding. Black smoke bellowed skyward as the fiberglass boat quickly burned to the very waterline, while still bobbing up and down in the wind-blown seas. In the midst of our near panic situation, the unexpected happened. Shrimp boats appeared from all directions. In less then ten minutes from the time we caught on fire, one shrimper was up beside the burning hull, vainly attempting to douse the inferno with his deck hose. Another shrimper scooped us up and had us safely on deck before we even had a chance to evaluate our situation. Even though we were somewhat stunned over the happenings, we were amazed that so many boats had responded so quickly. The captain of the boat that picked us up was N. J. Seymour out of Ocean Springs. He and his wife were shrimping on board their boat the "Doyle B", and actually saw it all happen. They immediately pulled in their nets and headed for us. Mrs. Seymour had the twins stripped of their wet clothes and all covered up in the bunk beds by the time I got my head together and started checking each one individually to make sure everyone was all right. Even though the temperature was well into the eighties, Gordon and I stood shaking in the pilot house doorway, silently thanking the All Mighty that we were all OK. About that time, as the remains of our craft started to sink slowly beneath the waves to join the rest of the sunken wreck, a Coast Guard helicopter suddenly appeared over us. Captain Seymour got busy on the radio, telling the Coast Guard and everyone else listening, that we were all safe and sound on the "Doyle B". He then took a reading on the exact location where our vessel had sunk and headed toward the Ocean Springs Harbor. I thought at the time that I bet every boat around, plus the 'chopper had also taken a reading on the spot. I knew for sure that I would need those coordinates by the time the accident investigation was over. By the time we got to port, the twins had consumed a bag of chips, two cookies apiece, a coke and still acted half starved, like nothing had even happened. However, as soon as we docked, they were ready to tell the world and anyone else that would listen, about their unexpected swim in the Mississippi Sound. We will always be grateful to Captain N. J. Seymour, who has since passed away, for his quick and unselfish response in our time of need. And for the kindness and loving care Mrs. Seymour gave to the twins, even though for ten year olds, they responded very admirably in an emergency situation. And the many other shrimpers and fishing boats that hurried to see if they could be of help, will always come to mind and remind me of my duty should I ever see someone in distress. But we all pay a special tribute to (the late) N. J. Seymour, Captain of the "Doyle B" and to his wife for their rescue that day that was, "A DAY TO REMEMBER".

A PERFECT DAY

Rain, rain and more rain. Days, weeks and months of rain filled skies kept even the most avid fishermen off the water for as long as two or three weeks, resulting in some severe cases of "cabin fever" throughout the South. When there was a rare sunny day, the wind blew hard and the seas ran rough, making it near impossible for any off shore fishing. But, as summer crowded into the end of the worst wet spring anyone could remember, things started to get better. A couple of days with light, variable winds and a few harmless scattered showers made a world of difference. By late June, folks were going crazy to get on the water. Thousands of fishermen jumped at the chance to enjoy man's second favorite past time while even the water-sport enthusiast literally tore up the bays and bayous, just boat riding and enjoying the great Mississippi Gulf Coast. Tomorrow was forecast to be A PERFECT DAY!! Even Mike Reader, Channel 13's popular TV weatherman had given a very favorable prognosis for at least the next 48 hours. The ever-reliable Keesler AFB weather forecaster unequivocally verified Mike's evening report. So, it didn't take too much coaxing to get a fishing trip going for the next day. As I packed my stuff that night before heading for bed, my excitement mounted. But that's not too unusual, as I still get that way before a long awaited fishing trip. It had been well over a month since I had even wet a line. I did, however, run out into the back yard between showers and make a few practice casts just to make sure that I still knew how. Now that's a true sign of cabin fever. When you see someone out in the yard casting on dry land, you know they either have a brand new fishing outfit or they have a sever case of too much time locked indoors. By the time that I settled down and slipped into bed, my wife Jacky, was sound asleep. Long after I turned out the lights however, I was still restless; changing the position of my pillow and rolling from one side to the other. Instead of counting sheep, I did a mental checklist of each and every item I intended to take with me in the morning. I was really annoyed that Jacky slept right through all my twisting and turning as no one likes to stay awake by themselves. Much later, half asleep, I even thought I heard thunder in the distance, and was dimly aware of a somewhat passive fear that it might be raining in the morning. The last thing I remembered was looking at the bright numbers on the clock radio and thinking that if I didn't get to sleep soon, I might just as well stay up the rest of the night.

Wow!! It seemed like only a few minutes had gone by when the irritating buzz of our alarm clock shattered the early morning silence. For some reason, I wasn't the least bit tired and was immediately wide awake and out of bed. Quickly dressing, I looked outside and was relieved to see a clear sky, filled with millions of twinkling stars. More stars than I ever remember seeing before, even during countless hours of night flying, miles above the earth, in the crystal clear atmosphere that I learned to love so much. Yes, it looked like Mike Reader was right. It was going to be A PERFECT DAY . . . .

Well, it didn't take long to load up and head out to pick up some of my old fishing buddies. This was really a very special trip for me. The main reason was because I had just gotten a great new boat that was big enough for us all to go. I had called all my old fishing buddies and invited everyone that could go. First, I was pick'n up Grady "If I never catch another fish", Cook, Dick "Goldfinger" Davis and Dick "Is everybody here happy?" Hoover. `Course a couple of other fishing buddies couldn't make it, like John "Mr. Outdoors Editor" Lambeth, as he had a bass tournament that weekend, and Mike "I sure do like White Trout" Chester, because he was busy gett'n ready for deer season. So the three Dicks and Grady headed for Wilson's Fishing Camp where I had my new boat docked. When we arrived, the other two members of my "select" fishing party were already there and had that eager look on their faces. Steve "I really would rather be playing golf" Muench, and Dick "Is the weather really OK. to go fishing?" Brown, were ready to go, so I told them all to pick up what ever they wanted to drink and get the ice while got the bait. Now everyone I fish with always jokes about my friend, Fred Deegan and his catch and release stories on 4 and 5 pound Specks he has caught on his special name-brand artificial lures. Then he keeps just enough "keepers" for supper and still marvels when folks use live bait successfully. As a bait camp owner and bait shrimper, I certainly would never go saltwater fishing without live shrimp, unless they were just not available. So, with the cold drinks iced down, the live bait aerated and all the tackle neatly stowed, we checked to make sure the skiffs were secure and headed South. I don't really remember much about the trip to Chandelier Island except that it seemed like it took no time at all and we were at our destination. Things were just happening. The best location was selected, the anchor secured, skiffs quickly put overboard and each loaded down with our fishing gear. I had long been decided who was fishing with who, by simply drawing numbers from a hat. Dick Davis and Dick Hoover were the first two names drawn and they had quickly loaded their skiff and were departing the area. Steve Muench and Dick Brown were in another skiff and that left the old man of the sea, Grady Cook, with me. Well, that made everyone happy with their partner, especially me, as Grady Cook is one good fisherman. As I climbed into the skiff with Grady, I checked my watch and could not believe that it was only 6:30 a.m. Everything was working like clock-work. Just perfect. We had all agreed to check back at the boat at noon for lunch and compare notes as to where the fish were and what bait they were caught on. Plus, to see who had caught the first, biggest and most so far. Of course, I had the live bait with me because no one else likes to mess with live shrimp out at Chandelier. But I do!! Of course, that was OK. with Grady too because we both have a lot of faith in natural bait and we just knew that live shrimp would catch the biggest and most. Grady would say "Look, if you got some God-given natural bait, use it!" Of course I can remember a lot of other famous Grady Cook quips about fishing but most are unprintable and would have to be censured to the point of losing their humor. But he spoke the truth this time.

As we skimmed across the grassy flats toward an area that Grady and I knew we could catch fish, I marveled at the beautiful, deep blue sky as it melted into the clear blue-green water to the west. But my daydreaming seemed to be suddenly interrupted by Grady motioning for me to slow down. Just ahead the grassy flats seemed to be polka-dotted with deep aqua-colored pockets, which were perfect hiding places for Mr. Speck and Mr. Redfish. I maneuvered the skiff to a point about 50 feet up-wind of the nearest hole and in no time what a beautiful live shrimp baited and ready to get our first fish. I quickly flipped the morsel to the far side of the dark area and gently popped the small cork, thinking that I would work it across the edge to the far side. But, what to my wondering surprise, the cork immediately disappeared, followed by a strong steady pull on the line and the fight was on. As I raised the rod tip high, I heard the 12 pound test line sing as it started to pull at the drag that I had pre-set for an average keeper. If this was a Speck, it certainly was not average, as I lowered my rod tip and readjusted my drag. Grady had not even wet a line yet, so you can imagine the side comments I was hearing from the other end of the boat. After about 30 yards of line had been given up, I began to get worried about all the grass that would be building up on the retrieve. I put a little more pressure on him, only to get a surge at the other end that took another 10 to 15 more yards of line. "Shark!" I thought, as I applied even more pressure. But, then again, by now a Shark or even a Spanish Mackerel would have cut the light mono line I was using with their sharp teeth. Then I felt the familiar head shake and was almost certain that it was a very respectable Red or one heck of a Speckled Trout. As we drifted across the hole and into the grass on the far side, I was rapidly gaining line. Suddenly the water literally exploded about 20 yards from the boat and for an instant the spotted tail of a beautiful Redfish appeared just above the surface. I'm not really sure just how I landed the popular Chandelier prize, or how long it took me in all that grass, but I do remember telling Grady to check the time so that we could report when the first fish was caught. I had just released my Red when Grady gave a grunt and started to softly speak to whatever he had just hooked into. Knowing Grady, I couldn't really tell by his actions if he had a trophy fish or an average school Speck. It didn't look like his tackle was reacting to a real buster, but once again, remember, you never really know what Grady Cook has on the other end until you see it or ask him. He tends to play them all the same. Very carefully and seldom loses a fish. Seeing someone else catch a nice fish is almost as much fun as catching one yourself . . . almost. The fish stayed right around the grassy hole and even though it made a few short runs, Grady had it whipped and into the boat within a few minutes. A very respectable 3 pound Speck. Our first fish in the box but certainly not our biggest or last. I could go on and on with a, blow by blow, description of our luck for the next two hours but I'm sure that it will suffice to say that we did well. And to make things even sweeter, when we arrived at the boat, we found that everyone had also done exceptionally well. Some had caught a few more than others and there were a few really nice sized Specks, but of course Grady and I had caught the biggest and the most. Gosh, I could hardly wait until the afternoon, cause so far, this was . . .

A PERFECT DAY.

I wasn't really all that hungry and as I set in the sun listening to all the others telling about the ones they missed, I guess I dozed off. Suddenly, someone was shaking me and saying, "Dick, get up! You're going to be late, as it's after 5:00 am. I thought that you were leaving at 5:00 sharp!!" The cobwebs cleared quickly as I suddenly realized that it was my wife, Jacky that was shaking me and telling me to wake up! I was still at home in my own bed. It had all been a wonderful dream. But, alas, I didn't really own a great new boat. I didn't really catch all those beautiful big Specks. I didn't really catch the biggest and the most. I didn't even really go fishing yet. But, as I got dressed and thought about my dream, I knew in my heart that I had just experienced A PERFECT DAY . . . .

LIVE AND LEARN

Grandpa Smith had come to town, all the way from Muncie, Indiana, and as usual, the very first item on his agenda was fishing. Never did make any difference where we lived, Florida, Indiana, Alabama, Texas, Nevada or Mississippi, when my father-in-law came to visit, we went fishing ASAP!! This year was no exception. As soon as he hit the door, his first question was, "Are they bittin'?" And as it turned out, he did have a fishing trip that will always be a most memorable one for Mr. Charles E. Smith, from the land of the "Hoosiers".

Now "Grandpa Charlie", as my kids respectfully address him, was a fun-loving, rough and tough, retired wire-worker that is still remembered by many old-time sportsmen around Muncie, as a rugged, "fair-to-midland", sandlot catcher on the local semi-pro baseball team. As the President of his local steel workers union, Grandpa Charlie had earned the respect and reputation as a fighter and arbitrator for the workingman. At times he wasn't really too easy on his son-in-law either. But, all I had to do is take him fishing and I was his favorite son-in-law. Course, I was his only son-in-law since my wife Jacky, had four brothers and no sisters. Well, Grandpa and Grandma Smith had arrived shortly after high noon, just as he had predicted so I was well prepared. Air Force buddy and fishing partner, (the late) Dick Davis was only a few minutes behind them, as he docked his trim little run-about at my pier behind the house. While Charlie and I unpacked their car, so he could change clothes and get ready, Dick and my youngest son, Marty, started to load the boat. Even with all the corners cut and hurrying as fast as we could, it was 3:30 p.m. by the time we were iced down, geared up and adequately fortified with all the bait and chum we could find, as we passed under the highway 90 bridge at the mouth of the historic Back Bay of Biloxi. Already the shadows were starting to lengthen as we set course for Ship Island, located about 8 miles South of the last Biloxi Ship Channel marker. It was apparent that the long summer days were starting to get shorter, but no problem, as it was during the late afternoon and early evening that we had been catching our best fish, which included big Speckled Trout around the rock pile and Bull Reds in the deeper waters in Little Dog Key Pass. We were primed and ready to get Grandpa Charlie into some great fishing in the Mississippi Sound. It was just about 5:00 p.m. by the time we actually got anchored on the South end of the 36 foot deep hole in Little Dog Key Pass and closer to 5:30 p.m. by the time that we finally set back and got ready to catch fish. We had set out four poles with the lines out in four different directions. Plus, a chum bag full of ripe thawed-out fish and other seafood leftovers, which left a beautiful "slick" almost half way back to Biloxi. Not knowing from one day to the next just what big Bull Reds might be feeding on, we had been taking fresh blue crab, Mullet, shrimp, squid and menhaden and often we would bait up with a little of each until we could tell just what they wanted. This method proved to be the right ticket this time also, as along about 6:30, after a frustrating hour of fighting hungry hardhead catfish, the ever familiar click, click, click, followed by a slow, hard run, soon had smiling and setting on the edge of his chair. With a quick upward motion, I set the hook firmly into whatever was trying to steal all my line. Confident that this was what we had came out there for, I quickly handed the rod to Charlie and quietly stated, "He's all yours Charlie!" Now Charlie is an experienced angler and no one had to tell him what to do. His face lit up like a young boy catching his first bass, and he immediately started to pump the rod and claim back line from what was hopefully his first Bull Red this year. After about five or six minutes of this, the fish began to tire, and it was shortly there after that the gallant fighter was lifted into the boat. Everyone congratulated Charlie on his nice 25 pound red and had no more then reset the line out again, when things really started to happen. As a matter of fact, during the next 30 minutes, each of us got our chance to hook up with our own hefty spot-tail. In the meantime, we got a real kick out of Charlie as he would barely get rested from the last tussle when someone would hand him a rod loaded with a fight'n red on the other end and say to him, "You all catch this one Charlie, and we'll get'cha another one."

By the time the sun was trying to hide itself behind the horizon and darkness was closing in around our happy little group, we had sixteen beautiful Bull Reds in the box, with a couple of them looking to be in the 30 pound class. But then, just about the time that we had all decided that we had enough and were getting ready to pull in the lines and head for the barn, two of the reels started releasing line at above average speed without the usual pre-warning click that the others had given. Thinking that it might possibly be Shark moving in, I set the hook hard and offered the rod to Charlie who quickly shook his head and refused saying, "Hell, you catch him, I'm tired! I know I've landed at least nine or ten of em' already." Everyone on board got a chuckle out of that and Dick Davis decided about that time that he better find out just what was taking out line on the other reel. When he set the hook I knew that he had a pretty good fish, as it didn't seem to slow down a bit. So I shrugged and started putting some back bone into the rod that I was still holding. I was suddenly greeted with a heavy tug, followed by a slow, hard run, unlike the swift line-taking run of a medium size Blacktip Shark. Would you believe it took me almost 15 minutes before I was able to gain most of my line back, however due to several hard head shakes that vibrated up the line and through the rod, I was convinced that it must be a super Bull Red. As the battle continued, I became concerned that maybe my 40 pound test mono-line might not be sufficient for the sawing like treatment it was receiving on the rough mouth of the red. I also felt that by now, a Shark would have cut it off. Most Bull Reds are initially hard fighters, but don't usually have too much stamina, especially if you have heavy fishing gear and can fight them aggressively. By this time, Dick Davis had his fish in the boat and it appeared to be the largest one so far. I became more anxious and began to force my fish even more. Within what seemed like several minutes, but was really only about 20 seconds, my increased efforts paid off as the huge Bull Red came to the surface just to the rear of the boat. Everyone cheered and pointed, as this was by far, the biggest catch of the day. As I reeled the exhausted fighter to the boat, I requested the stainless steel gaff and handed the rod to Dick. Carefully, but swiftly, I pulled the sharp tip of the gaff through the lower lip and quickly hauled my beauty on board. Though totally exhausted, he gave one last flip and then laid perfectly still on the floor of the boat as I removed the 3/0 hook. It was truly a beautiful specimen, as the deck light exposed it's bright reddish-orange color, broken only by the typical dark spot located back near the tail fin. For a moment, a wave of sorrow swept over me, knowing that life was over, however the vision of it mounted over my fireplace quickly took its place. Seeing the two large fish still laying on the floor of the boat must have really motivated Marty as he quickly baited one of the rods and threw right back into the same area as the last two were caught. When I told him that we really needed to head for home, he gave me his typical reply, "Just one more and we'll go, or even if I just lose my bait, OK Pop?" Well, he got his request answered before I could even reply, as he reared back and set the hook. By the time he had landed his, we had two more on the other two lines that were set out the other side of the boat. Well, that did it!! We had a grand total of 21 reds and bait, blood and tackle all over the boat. The big ice chests were full and there were several fish in the deck wells as we pulled up anchor and headed north. We kiddingly asked Grandpa Charlie if he wanted to go someplace else to catch some really big Shark, to which he quickly replied with a big grin, "No!! Hell, I'm tired, you guys wore me out! I know I caught most of them. I think I probably caught the biggest one too." He said as he looked at me with a twinkle in his eye. What an evening. 21 big Bull Reds! And some of them were over the 40 pound mark. But wait a minute!! The law says only three fish per person, which is a total of only 12 reds between the four of us and what about only being able to keep one red per person over 30 inches?

Well, this is a true story that happened just as described, but in the fall of 1974, on board a little 19 foot run-about owned by Dick Davis, who was then a Col. in the USAF. Yes, this actually happened over 17 years ago when there were no laws or regulations to protect many of our great sport fish of the Gulf of Mexico. Sport fishermen, charter boats and commercial fishermen were all encountering large schools of "Bull Reds" and literally filling their boats on a daily basis. I was really no different. Many a night I cleaned Red Fish until nearly midnight. I not only filled my freezer, but would give away five to six fish a trip. I remember nearly choking when someone would ask, "Are they cleaned?" Needless to say, they never got called again for any free fish. But I can truthfully say, we never wasted or sold a fish commercially. Of course if it is only fair to admit that at the time, the big Bull Red was really hard enough to give away, let alone sell it. Not too long after this trip, I started to hear a saying that became popular among the saltwater fishermen during the next few years. Many times you would hear, "Save the Buffalo", over the radio while out fishing the waters south of the barrier islands. By 1976, several of the more conservative charter boat captains picked up the chant and were establishing self imposed creel limits per trip. By the mid 1980's, the Gulf Coast Conservation Association was screaming for new creel and size limits in the Gulf, for it appeared that some of our marine fisheries population was rapidly being depleted. By the late 1980's, regulations stiffened and new, more restrictive creel and size limits were established. In the case of some fish, it was almost too late, especially for the Bull Red. Today, more and more anglers are practicing catch and release programs, even when the fish exceeds the minimum size. Yes, we LIVE AND LEARN. As great as our huge saltwater marine fisheries may appear, we are finally learning that we can over-fish a given species, if we do not impose regulatory control. Local anglers well remember the days when it was a relatively common sight to see acres and acres of Bull Reds feeding on the surface all throughout our beautiful Mississippi Sound. Now, only those who fish on a regular daily bases still run into a few of the big schools where the water looks like it is turning orange. Yes, the blackened Red Fish also took it's toll, and the purse net violations where hundreds of thousands of pounds of reds were rounded up and sold to the commercial market. The price of Red Fish seemed to skyrocket in a matter of months. Things really changed. As a reminder of the "good old days", I still have my big Red Fish from that eventful trip mounted and displayed above my fireplace. The magnificent species weighed 46 pounds and was 44 inches in length. Like many other anglers that I have heard about since, I never checked the existing state record, which was then and is still today, 44 pounds and 11 ounces. I only know it was a great fish and I wanted to get it mounted. How many reds over 40 pounds do we catch today in our surrounding waters? Think about it!!

Even Grandpa Charlie, who is now 83 years old and still shares fond memories of that trip, is well aware that we continue to LIVE AND LEARN about our great natural resources. Let's hope that, today's and tomorrow's generation will continue to LIVE AND LEARN so that our grandchildren, their grandchildren and your grandchildren can still catch the big Bull Red.

JUST ME

I couldn't help but wonder if maybe I had made a mistake in judgment as I quietly turned off the alarm clock and retreated back into the warmth of the heavy comfort that spread like a giant umbrella over our queen-size bed. There certainly was little doubt that the outside air temperature had made a sizable drop for the third night that week, as even our bedroom felt cold. It appeared that my friend, the weather forecaster for our local TV station, had made a good call as the temperature had to be near or below freezing. I think it was Shakespeare that wrote "TO BE OR NOT TO BE, THAT IS THE QUESTION." Well at this point, Dick Wilson was thinking, "TO GO OR NOT TO GO, THAT IS THE QUESTION"! You guessed it! To go fishing . . . or not to go fishing. And to make this decision more personal and difficult, it was entirely up to me, 'cause I was going alone. JUST ME. Not by choice, mind you, but only because I could not find anyone that could (or would) go. My hand-full of die-hard fish'n buddies were all tied up with domestic chores or hunt'n or something, and my not so die-hard fishing friends all seemed to come up with a million reasons why they could not go. Personally, I think it all boiled down to creature comfort. Better known as "Just too damned cold". Some were pretty honest about it and told me that I must be crazy. But, you got to understand, I had the day off. So there you have it! I had watched the weather, listened to the news and was even believing the great fish stories I had been hearing all week. I just couldn't stand it any longer and I was going even if the Gulf was frozen over!!! I work a lot of weekends and since this was a slow week, I had requested the day off. But, at that moment, with no one to answer to but myself, the outside temperature in the low 30's and my better judgment saying to roll over, snuggle in and go back to sleep, I really did some self-motivating. The longer I laid there, the more determined I became and finally, fully awake, I slipped from beneath the covers and into my long-johns. By the time I had brushed my teeth and completed all the normal early morning get-up and go chores, I was warmed up and anxious to get on the road.

One of my real faithful fish'n partners, Grady Cook, was already committed to a two day trip over in Louisiana, but when he found out that I was look'n to go "Speck" fishing up the Tchoutacabouffa River, he very graciously offered me his 15 foot skiff. I took him up on his offer and already had it hitched to my number one fish,n vehicle and all I needed to do was load up and go launch the boat. Since I was just going up the river, I stopped at Popps Ferry Fishing Camp and picked up some live shrimp. As usual, Rea Gensert loaded me up with a very generous count,(She seldom counts, just gives you a bunch.) Being a fishing camp owner, I know what's a bunch of shrimp. Even though it was just breaking daylight as I approached the proclaimed "promised land", I could pick out the shape of at least five other boats already in position. But, the little lake like cove had ample room for several more boats and usually during the week, especially on very cold mornings, only the true die-hards are out. So, being fairly familiar with the area, and knowing where I had caught fish in previous years, I quietly let out a couple of trolling lines and slowly moved up along the Northeast side of the cove to a point where the bottom slops up from about 25 feet to a 5 foot bar. As I passed the first of three points that stick out into the cove, I got my first strike. I liked to jumped out of my seat as I grabbed for the rod that was now bent nearly double even with the drag silently releasing line. The pull was so steady that at first I thought that I had gotten too close to the shore and hung-up on the bottom. But then I felt that familiar hard jerk that usually is indicative of a good fish. I immediately set the hook for good measure and cut the trolling motor off. Within a minute or so, silver beauty surfaced behind the boat and I nervously glanced around for the landing net, knowing that this one was a little too big to swing into the boat. As the distance between us narrowed, my adrenalin started to overpower my better judgment and just that quick I realized that I was forcing the fish too much. Too late I saw that I did not have the fish hooked good. And, since I had forced the fish in too quickly, it simply gave a last ditch head shake and threw the hook. Believe me, that was such a smooth catch and release of a "5 pounder" that Fred Deegen would have been proud. I was shaken but not destroyed, as that was not the first, nor will it be the last nice fish lost, just seconds from the landing net or gaff. As I begin to retrieve the unattended starboard line, which was now running all the way under the boat, I felt a hard jerk, to which I responded with a harder jerk. Much to my surprise but total delight, the rod was nearly jerked out of my hands as it bent sharply under the boat. As I set the hook I leaned far over the side to ensure that the line was not cut or frayed on the bottom of the boat. Carefully playing out the line, I moved to the front of the boat with visions of a real trophy-size Speck dancing through my head. This one was really shaking his head and had the weight of big fish. As the minutes dragged by, I started having doubts, like maybe I had just snagged an average fish by the tail. I just wasn't gaining any line and at times it felt like a log. Finally, as I gained enough line to be directly over the fish I saw the long, tubular shaped culprit about 3 feet down. You guessed it! A big old alligator gar had found my shrimp just sitt'n on the bottom and I guess I set the hook before he had a chance to swallow it. Otherwise, he could have easily slashed the light mono-line with his razor-sharp teeth. But, no such luck. This hangover from the prehistoric days was firmly hooked in the hard part of his mouth, with the line well free of the toothy area. Not wanting to mess with him for obvious reasons, I cut the line down near his mouth as I dared. Great!! My second catch-and-release for the day. My buddies in GCCA would really be proud of me now. After replacing the hook, I picked out a couple of frisky live shrimp and started to troll back to the area again. By this time it was full daylight and I counted seven other boats within at least 100 yards of me. As I maneuvered back over my favorite spot near the deep water point, I noticed some of the other boats were headed that way too. Obviously they had seen my recent battle with the last two fish I had hooked and probably thought this dumb dude had just lost two nice fish. Well, I guess they were half right anyway. Not really wanting to share my spot, I just moved to the top of the drop-off and gently let down my anchor. Picking up the third rod already rigged with a popp'n cork, I quickly baited with another nice big shrimp and cast out the front of the boat. I retrieved the other two lines and was just re-rigg'n one when I saw my cork suddenly disappear. I reeled in the slack line and swiftly set the hook. Almost immediately the fish came flopping to the surface. As I played the fish closer to the boat, the line suddenly reversed and the lightly set drag respectfully and gently resisted the last surge for freedom. Determined to land my first catch of the day, I scooped the tired Fish up with the landing net just as soon as it was within reach. Not nearly as big as the first one, but when your fish-hungry, a two and a half pounder looks pretty good.

Encouraged with this action, I re-baited and sent corks shooting out in two different directions off the point. Almost immediately one of the corks disappeared and as soon as I set the hook I knew it was a small school Trout. Remembering what Sun-Herald Outdoors Editor, John Lambeth had written about catch and release methods, I quickly wet my towel and gently grasp the fish to remove the hook. Since it was only hooked in the mouth I had little problem extracting the hook and releasing the fish. Actually, John and I have caught literally hundreds of fish and only kept enough to improve our freezer stock. Suddenly, my daydream was shattered, as I nearly got my rod taken away from me. I hadn't noticed that the other cork was nowhere in sight. I reeled in the slack and set the hook hard. Wow, it was like set'n the hook on a log! The thought crossed my mind, "Oh no, not another ugly old gar". But then the fish began to run a little and shake his head a lot like a five pound Red Fish will do. My interest picked up real quick. I played the fish like it was the last fish I'd ever catch, and after about three or four minutes, I got my first glimpse of what looked like the biggest Trout I'd ever caught. Then I really got excited. I don't care if I catch a million fish, I hope I never get over the thrill of hook'n up with a nice fish. I took in some line and then I'd lose some line, and it really was a lot of fun, but I kept thinking about the one that got away when I first started to fish that morning. Finally, I felt the pressure reduce some and then a lot as the fish began to swim slowly toward me. Expecting a last life saving run, I checked my drag to make sure I wouldn't screw up this time. But to my amazement, as the fish was retrieved beside the boat, it turned on it's side and never made a move until it was laying in the bottom of the boat with its gills gasping from the exhausting battle. Later I weighed the fish in at a shade over 6# 12 oz. Not the biggest Trout I've ever caught, but it sure did look good in my little 48 qt. cooler. Still excited and eager to catch me a few more, I concentrated on just one cork to watch. Much to my dismay, no matter how much popp'n and twitch'n of the cork I did, nothing else happened. Finally, I got the message and checked my bait. Sure enough, sometime during the heat of the battle with my catch-of-the-day, a little ol' bait stealer had done a job on me. So, I re-baited and this time I just flipped it out there where I had caught the big one. Sure didn't have to wait long on this one because the cork never stopped when it hit the water. It was no task to set the hook however, and required even less effort to reel it in, as this one was not even 10 inches long. Well, the next three fish were also in the undersized category and released in good health, however that was enough to make me give serious thought about moving. But, about that time, I hooked into another nice fish. This one was about the same size as the first one that I had put into the cooler. For the next two hours I continued to catch fish and by about 10:45 I had caught and released nearly two dozen little shakers, but had about 10 or 12 real nice keepers, and that was plenty for me. The catch'n was starting to slow down and by this time there were some folks darn near fishing in my boat. I gently lifted the anchor and slowly maneuvered out of the cove to head for the house. I suddenly realized that it was not really that cold and I had a real nice day. As I looked at my catch for the morning, I just couldn't help but feel elated that I had decided to get up and go even if it was freezing temperature and JUST ME . . . .

FRUSTRATED

The weather was extremely poor for fishing off shore and at the time I didn't even own a skiff to fish the bays and bayous. Just as soon as the new year came in, I started to look around for that great bargain that usually appears in the boats for sell section of the paper along about that time of year. When money gets tight, you can scan the ads in the newspaper and find just about anything that you want. I looked at dozens of boats during the following weeks and it seemed that what sounded like a good deal turned out to be junk or if it really was a good deal, someone had just beat me to it. Finding a boat that you like and meets your limited financial criteria can really be difficult sometimes. But, finally I found one that really seemed like a good deal and I liked the rig. It was a nice clean little 16' Fiberglas Starcraft, small console, depth recorder and powered by a 35 hp Johnson outboard with a trailer that looked great. The seller had just taken it in on a trade in and advised that he had not really had a chance to fool with it, therefore he would let it go at the bargain price. Everything looked good. The boat was in good shape and clean as a pin, rigged to go fish'n right now! The engine fired up with a turn of the key and appeared to run well. Shifted easily into gear and idled down to a purr. It had a steel prop that was in excellent condition and the outer appearance of the housing was good. The trailer did need a new buddy bearing on the portside, otherwise I was satisfied that the rig would serve the purpose for fishing the bay, bayous and even along the front beach. I did however have to purchase the rig, "as is". That is usually always a mistake!! And I know better! No warranty . . . . and as is!! I guess my "cabin fever" clouded by judgment, or I must have figured that the price was good enough that I could afford any minor repairs I might encounter. But, I just blundered right on through with the deal and in a matter of a few minutes I was heading down the road with my "new boat" following right behind. Well the weather delayed the first opportunity for a maiden voyage, so it was several days before I put the boat in the water for the first time. Friday afternoon, just as soon as I got home from work, I changed clothes and was in the water within 20 minutes of getting home. As I hoped, the engine cranked up immediately and I was a happy boat owner, for a short time. I had called an old fish'n buddy, Dick Hoover, and told him that I was making a trial run and if he wanted to go along, I'd be up to his home on the Tchoutacabouffa River in about 15 minutes. As I pulled up to his dock, I thought that I noticed the engine didn't seem to want to idle just right as I shifted into reverse. But I didn't really give it too much thought at the time. Dick even brought along his fish'n gear, cause knowing me, he figured that we would look for a little action while we were trying out the motor. Somewhere along about 4-Jacks area, the motor began to slow down and by the time we were almost to Oak Lawn, it was down to idle and only hitting on one plug. I did a 180 degree turn and headed back to Dick's house. Needless to say, it took us almost twice as long to get back as to get there, so I just dropped off Dick and headed for home before it got dark. As soon as I got to the boat launch, it was still light enough to see, so I took off the motor cover and the only thing I could see that didn't look right was the carburetor throat was wide open and very wet with fuel like the engine was flooding. Well I put the cover on, loaded the boat on the trailer and headed for the house.

The first thing that I did when I got home was to put in new plugs, as one was really fouled up badly. Then I checked the automatic choke and it seemed to be sticking. I then sprayed some WD-40 on it and it seemed to work better. I hooked up the water and the engine came to life as soon as I turned the key. I played around with it for a few minutes and satisfied that the plug had just gone bad, I put the cover back on and called it a night. Grady Cook called me that night and I told him what had happened and that I needed to make another shake-down run the next day. We decided that we would wait until mid-morning just in case I had not found the cause of my problem. So, about 10:00 o'clock the next morning we were motoring up the river like nothing was ever wrong. But not very far!! Once again, the engine cut back to a rough speed and then to idle. This time, it really sounded bad. I guess I had not learned my lesson the first time as I didn't bring along a plug wrench or spare plugs this time either, so we just limped back to the boat launch. As soon as we got to a phone, we called the boat doctor that Grady knew might still be open. They stated that they were normally open just until noon, however they would stay open for us. Hurry!! True to their word, they were still there when we arrived at about 12:45. I could not help but be impressed with all the attention that we received and it was quickly determined that there was a broken wire from the power pack and another small electrical part was bad. Within about an hour, they had the part replace, engine tuned and we were heading for home. By now it was mid-afternoon and we decided that we would call it a day. If the weather was O.K. we would try again in the morning. It was dark and early when I talked to Grady the next morning and it was mutually agreed upon that the weather forecast did not look very good, so we called off the trip. The wind was still blowing pretty good and it looked like rain. Along about 8:00 o'clock, he called me and said he still had a "hanker'n" to go fish'n and had I looked outside lately? Well, to make a 10 minute phone call short, he wanted to know if I wanted to go over to Lake of Pines and Spring Lake in Jackson County to fish for some green Trout. I guess I was still suffering from a relapse of cabin fever and somewhat disappointed in my own boat problem, because I quickly responded favorably and away we went. Well, the weather really got nice and by the time we got back to good old Biloxi, it was so nice that we decided to check out my boat. We transferred our equipment from his boat to mine and headed for the launch ramp, thinking that at least we could fish until dark. The launch was uneventful and the engine cranked immediately. We headed up the river, and this time we didn't even get past Wick's Fishing Camp before we dropped off to idle. All you boat owners know just how I felt, because if you have ever owned a used boat and motor or been around them very often, you have to just keep working to get the bugs out. Well, back to the drawing board.

About mid-week, I rushed home from work, hooked up the trailer and headed for the boat doctor again. This time I was just going to leave the boat with them. About a block from my destination, I felt the boat swerve a little and looking into my side-view mirror, I was horrified to see the wheel on the port side about to come off!! It started to wobble so badly that the trailer was jumping all over the road. Fortunately, I was at an intersection where there was a service station and I was able to pull in and stop before a dangerous situation became a total catastrophe. I asked the manager if I could leave the boat and trailer for a few minutes while I went for help. Angry over my misfortune but pleased that I had not lost the wheel and wrecked the boat, I drove on to the boat doctor. Upon arrival, I explained my dilemma and without hesitation, the mechanic picked up his tools, grabbed a small floor jack and we headed to the rescue. Examination of the faulty wheel revealed that all but one of the lug nuts had backed out leaving only the one holding the tire in place. It was a simple task to replace the four missing lug nuts and we headed for the shop.

After about a half hour of checking and rechecking, the boat doctor gave me the bad news. He advised me that I had a very sick motor and to get well it would require a new automatic choke and that it appeared to have a bad reed-valve. With a deep sigh and visions of my hard earned dollars flying across the waters, I approved the repairs and headed for home.

A few days later, the boat doctor called and stated that the repairs were made and to come pick up the boat. That evening, I hurried home from work to go get the boat as the next day was Saturday and I wanted to go fishing. What else ?? They cranked up the motor several times and it really sounded great. Needless to say, the bill was great too. But all marine repair bills are usually higher then you expect. Everything seemed legitimate, so I paid the bill and headed for the house.

Once again, Grady and I headed out to fish the waters of the Biloxi Back Bay and all the bayous and tributaries. This time we got a late start on Saturday due to the threat of rain and bad weather. About 11:00 am, we launched at the I-110 bridge boat ramp and headed toward Wilson's Fishing Camp for some bait. We didn't even make it to the railroad bridge when it became obvious that the motor was starting to do the same thing. Just prior to it dropping all the way to idle, I made a 180 degree turn and headed back the ramp. I couldn't believe it!! I looked at Grady and after stating a few of my favorite, well-worn words of anger and descriptive vernacular, I shook my head and vowed never again. Now I'm frustrated and mad. It was 2:00 p.m. by the time we got the boat back on the trailer and were heading back to the house. The bad part was that there was no boat doctor until Monday as he closes at noon Saturday and does not open until the following Monday morning.

Monday morning finally came and I called bright and early to state my displeasure and frustration. Not known for being real patient, I was somewhat proud of the way that I calmly handled the matter, for down deep I was really upset. I was pleased and relieved that the owner was extremely courteous and professional. He chuckled knowingly and just said to bring it in at my earliest convenience and they would do everything they could to make it well. So, once again, the first chance I got, down the road to the boat doctor I went. The very next day he called me and talked to me like I was the father of a very sick child. Seems that, sometime, way back when, our patient had almost passed into outboard happy hunting ground, however some quack boat doctor had put a Band-Aid fix on a near fatal wound and now it was seriously ill again. When they tore down the engine this time, they found the real culprit and source of my trouble. The engine had a cracked block behind the starter, had been welded and since the starter mounts were located in that area, it just didn't hold up. The starter bracket was even mounted wrong and the bolts had wallowed in the thread holes. Now I'm really FRUSTRATED. My fantastic bargain had now turned into an expensive nightmare. Dreading the answer, I then asked the BIG question. How much to make it well, or should I just walk away. Once again, I was impressed with the bedside manners of my boat doctor, as he truly felt bad about the situation and advised that if it were him, he would keep the engine and that he would repair it for me at what he felt was a very good price. Of course I related to him that I was somewhat leery of bargains at this time and I would have to think it over for a day or two, but in reality, what else could I do. The total repair bill was still only a fraction of the cost for a new engine. So, the next day I called and told him to go for it. But, that's not the end of the story.

Still without a boat, my cabin fever got even worse as it mixed in with my frustration. My better judgment was once again clouded by impatience and that insane desire to get out and go fishing. By force of habit, I scanned the boat sell ads and spotted a couple of new ones up for sell. Having nothing to do the very next Saturday, I went out and looked at boats. Same story. Some were just junk, some were great boats, but over priced, some were already sold and a couple I liked. I guess I'll know what I'm going to do when the sick one gets well and I can get out on that water again. By the time this story is in print, you can bet money that I am either one happy boat owner or just plain FRUSTRATED!!

GET RICH ON JACKS

The gentle breeze out of the southwest was just enough to create a slight ripple across the surface of the blue-green water of the Mississippi Sound. We had departed the Biloxi Small Craft Harbor at one minute past six a.m. and it was nearly six-forty a.m. by the time we had passed through Camille Cut and were moving smoothly to the South of Ship Island. The color of the water had changed dramatically from dull brown inside the barrier island to a sparkling, deep-water look that normally is not found so close in. I was openly pleased and silently relieved to see that the seas had calmed so rapidly following nearly a full week of ragging winds and booming thunderstorms all along the entire coast. Amazing as it was, it appeared that we were going to have a beautiful day. My brother-in-law, Michael Joe Smith, more commonly known as just plain "Smitty" by his Air Force friends, was back in Biloxi for a short visit. Mike had driven down from Indiana with his friend and business associate, Rich Mattmann, a talented young entrepreneur that had helped Mike get started in an amazing new business. Well, it didn't take much to convince me that we ought to take Rich fishing, especially when I learned that he had never caught a fish in his entire life. So here we were, heading out to the wild deep yonder with the mission for the day to get Rich hooked up with a big ol' Shark, Cobia, red, jack or even a frisky Bonito. The only limitation that we had was time as they had to be in at noon for a business appointment and we should not be going off shore too far in my little 19 foot Aquasport anyway. I started looking for a shrimp boat as we cleared the end of Ship Island and was not disappointed, as there were two or three in the distant horizon. As I headed for the closest one, which was still about a mile or two off Chandelier light, I couldn't help but hear part of the conversation between Mike and Rich. All I could make out however, was "Network" this and" Network" that, whatever that meant, but they sure were excited about it. Then I thought they were talking about fishing as I heard Rich tell Mike that in this business, you either had to fish or cut bait. This was a term that I was very familiar with and I thought at the time that this was not bad jargon for a guy that claims to have never caught a fish before. Seems however, that they were talking about a different kind of fish'n but whatever it was I interrupted them to explain a little about what we were going to do. With that, I directed their attention to the big double-rig steel hull that was now only a mile ahead of us. I could just visualize us being lucky enough to get into a school of Mackerel, Bonito, Jack Crevalle, or even really get lucky and hook up with a big old Cobia or Blacktip Shark. I crossed my fingers as I reduced the power about a half-mile out and after coming out of gear, I quickly begin to rig up three rods. I didn't really know just what to expect, so I rigged three different weight and size rigs. One, a relatively light 6 1/2 foot Berkley Sea Stick rod with 30 pound test mono line on an Ambassador 9000. One was a 6 1/2 foot Penn Rod of medium weight with a 4/0 Penn Senator and 40 pound test mono. The third rod, commonly known as the "BROOM STICK", was an ancient green 6 foot, heavy duty true temper rod with a big ol' 6/0 penn reel loaded with hundreds of yards of 80 pound test dacron line . . . . So, with a bucket full of chum, some great looking fresh bait fish and a lot of necessary tackle, I was confident that we could pull something out from under the big shrimp boat . . . . hopefully a big, fat Cobia. As I maneuvered into position just a few feet off the stern of the big steel hull, I caught the flashes of some large fish about 10 feet below the surface. My excitement quickened and I told Mike to grab a handful of chum and throw it up behind the boat while I came out of gear and handed the broom stick to Rich. For his first fish, I decided it best to stack all the cards in his favor. Even then, I know this first encounter would be plenty sporty. About the time the handful of chum hit the water, I tossed the baited line over the side and as I handed Rich the pole, I told him to hang on tight cause he was fix'n to hook up with a freight train. I also added that if he lost the rod overboard, the code of the seas was that he follow right behind it. Not really . . . . however it sure got his attention as he suddenly got a white-knuckled death grip on the rod. Well, the chum and the baited hook had hardly hit the water when a school of the biggest Jack Cravelle I have ever seen boiled and literally jumped out of the water in a sudden feeding frenzy. Suddenly, the big green broomstick bent in a 30 degree arch as the strong downward thrust of a large Jack grabbed the bait at near mach 1 and headed south. Caught by surprise, Rich was jerked to the very edge of the boat before he regained his footing and put his heart and back into just hanging on. All at once, the line moved from straight out in front to down the side of the boat to the stern. I quickly suggested to Rich to move to the rear of the boat with the fish and then followed to make sure that he would clear the outboard engine if the fish so decided to go on around the boat. The look of shear terror mixed with a little grin of absolute delight that showed on his face was worth the whole trip. As the line continued to peel off the big old reel and the pole bucked and bent in protest of the abuse it was taking, Rich looked up at me and said, "What do I do now, Coach?" I simply replied, "Hang on Rich, your turns coming." But, I'm not sure that Rich believed me as for the next 5 minutes there was still doubt as to who had who. Then suddenly, the line went almost limp and I saw the line start to run parallel with the boat making it possible for Rich to gain back some line, however at that minute Rich seemed to be still just hanging on, thankful for the reprieve. I quickly, and not too calmly advised him to reel in line as rapidly as he could and try to catch up with the fish as it was running toward him. Rich reeled so fast his hand was a blur and as he caught up with the fish and it felt the pressure, it turned 90 degrees and made another run away from our boat. This time straight for the shrimp boat, which was now thankfully, about 200 feet away. As the line now started to move rapidly toward the bow of the boat, Rich started to scrabble forward as I encouraged him to hang on, keep reeling and keep as much pressure on the fish as he could. Fortunately, with the antennas down in my little open fisherman, Rich was able to move to the bow with little effort, especially with the help of the fish half dragging him forward. This time Rich was able to turn the fish before very much line was lost, but now he had to change his tactics, as the Jack had turned sideways to our boat and began to sound. I explained to Rich what was happening and that now he would have to tire the fish by pumping the rod and reeling in as much line as he could as quickly as possible between pumps. In what seemed like just a minute or two, Rich had the bull nosed beauty to within about twenty feet of the boat, but still pulling sideways and about 10 feet deep. About that time, Mr. Jack saw the boat and made the typical last ditch effort to rejoin the school. But this time Rich was ready for him and it became obvious now, who had who. As the heroic fighter turned on it's side and was pulled along side the boat, I gently hooked the gaff into his lower lip, quickly removed the hook and released it all in a matter of seconds. Rich stared in disbelief, as the trophy that he had just spent moocho time and energy on flipped it tail and headed back toward the shrimp boat. I turned to Rich, shook hands with him and explained to him that Jacks were really not a very good food fish and therefore were usually always released to fight again. When I asked him how it felt to be a real deep sea fisherman, while still short of breath and recovering his strength, I heard him reply something about that he would be glad to cut bait while someone else caught the next one. Of course he was only kidding, for by the time I had re-baited, motored back to the shrimp boat and handed the rod to Mike, he appeared to be fully recovered and ready to be an active spectator. This time he offered to chum while Mike was on the catcher's end to the rod. Well, it didn't take long for Mike to get hooked up and the fun was on. Much to the delight of Rich, Mike made his trips around the boat, however since Mike used to live here on the gulf coast, he boated and released his fish a little faster than Rich. I then offered the rod back to Rich, however he insisted that I catch one while they rested. Knowing that they wanted the last laugh, I too used the broomstick, knowing that if I jerked the Jack's head up early, I could boat him in less than half the time that they had taken. Fortunately, that's the way it happened and I soon had the rod back into Rich's hands. I could go on and on telling about the fun we had catching and releasing Jacks as fast as our strength would allow us, and each time I approached the shrimp boat, I kept hoping to see a big old lemon, but to no avail. Numerous Jacks later, and as the little hand on my Mickey Mouse passed the eleven a.m. position, we stowed the gear and headed toward Camille Cut and Biloxi. As I glanced across at Mike and Rich, they were both quietly smiling as they gazed out across the beautiful water that extend to our sandy beaches on the Mississippi Gulf Coast. Much to our delight, we had fulfilled our mission to "GET RICH ON JACKS"!!!!

TAKE A KID FISHING

The very first hint of daylight was just starting to make its' appearance as I tip-toed in to the adjoining bedroom and gently tickled the little bare foot of my 5 year old grandson. A faint smile formed on his lips as his sleep filled eyes slowly opened. Then, as if stuck by a pin, he sat straight up in bed and in a rather loud, excited voice asked. "Is it time to go fish'n Papaw Dick?" "Shhhhh!", I cautioned him. "If you wake up the whole family, we will never get out of here!" "Grab your clothes and you can dress in the bathroom, while I fix you a bowl of cereal." Well, I didn't have to tell Blake Adcock anything twice when it came to going fishing. Of course, I don't know where he gets that from, but I do know that every time he comes to visit us here on the Coast, he expects to go fish'n with Papaw Dick. By the time I had his breakfast ready, he had washed the sleep out of his eyes, brushed his teeth and made a quick comb through his hair. He quickly gulped down his food, looked up at me with a big smile, and said, "Let's go, Papaw!"

In a matter of minutes, we had grabbed the sandwiches that Mamoo Jacky, (Blake's Grandmother) had made for us the night before, finished loading the skiff with last minute fishing gear, and were headed down the road. We had only gone a few blocks and I noticed that I was talking to myself, as Blake was already half asleep. However, as we parked in front of Wilson's Fishing Camp to pick up some live shrimp, he raised up enough to look out an ask, "Are we there already, Papaw?" Morris Sekul, who had leased the camp from yours truly, met us at the live bait tank and after filling our bait bucket with the lively little critters, he advised that they were catching Specks, White Trout, Ground Mullet and a few nice Reds on the oyster reefs. Blake quickly told him that Sheephead and Drum were also fun to catch, but he sure didn't like those Hardhead Catfish.

The sun was just starting to come up in the East and the tide was still moving as we silently slipped in the anchor at one of our favorite fishing spots. I put a live shrimp on Blake's hook and with one smooth cast he was ready to fish. I rigged my line with a popping cork and Blake had preferred to fish on the bottom with a light sinker. My cork just hit the water when it bobbed once and then went under. As I set the hook, I realized that it was a small fish. So happened that I then caught the next two fish, but they were also "Bradley size" Specks and I quickly release them. Even though they were too small to keep, this did not sit well with Mr. Blake. So I told him to reel in and I would put a cork on his line also. Just as I handed his rod back to him, I felt a strong tug on my rod and the cork was nowhere to be seen. I didn't even have to take up the slack. As I set the hook, Blake yelled out, "Catch him, Papaw". I raised the tip of the rod high and felt the strength of the fish as it shook its head and pulled a little drag. After a minute or two, we saw a faint flash of orange splash the surface and the fight was over. A nice 4 to 5 pound Redfish popped into our cooler shortly thereafter. Just about that time, Blake let out a squeal and yelled, "Papaw Dick, I got one too". I immediately laid down my rod and gave my full attention to the front of the boat where Blake appeared to be having the time of his life. Between grunts and squeals of joy, it appeared he was winning the battle, when all at once his line went slack. "Reel, Blake, reel!" I advised, with a raised voice. "The fish is running towards you!" Blake was near tears, as he thought his fish had gotten off; but just that quick, his line straightened out towards the side of the boat, with such force, it nearly pulled the rod out of his hands. As his drag squealed in protest, and his pole nearly bent double, Blake hung on for dear life. Eventually, the fish turned back toward the stem of the boat and the fight was on! Finally, it appeared that the fish was tiring and coming in with each turn of the reel handle. By this time I was starting to suspect that it was not a Redfish or a big old Speck. But I still grabbed the net and moved up next to Blake, ready to put it in the boat.

As the fish drew near the boat a 4 to 5 inch fin broke the surface and Blake asked between grunts, "What is it Papaw'?" At that second, the fish made a slow shallow pass right next to the boat and I made a lucky downward dip with the net just in time to scoop it up and swing it into the boat. "Papaw, You got him!" exclaimed Blake, as I quickly threw the four foot Blacktip Shark into the 100 Qt. cooler. Now, I had a "happy camper" on board. Well that was the start of a fun filled morning, with Blake catching the lion's share of the fish, while Papaw was busy keeping him baited up, changing hooks and opening the cooler every time he swung a "keeper" on board. By noon, Blake had just about all the sun and fun his little body could handle, as he was flat tuckered out. As we headed back to the boat dock, I could not help but think back to when my three sons, Steve, Mike and Marty, were small and all the hours we spent together fishing and competing each trip as to who caught the biggest and most. Today, that has not changed, as the four of us cherish the times we all can get together and spend a day, fishing. Yes, as I look back to these many years of fishing with my boys and grandsons, I know in my heart, that it's a good investment in tomorrows' future to "Take A Kid Fishing"!

GETTING BETTER

When the winds are calm and the heat from the mid-day sun is intense and nearly unbearable, we tend to forget those few miserable, cold and wet days that put limits upon our fishing during the otherwise relatively mild winter months. For some, a few days of this cold, wet weather can produce severe cabin fever, watching each report for a good forecast and just not very good company to anyone. While for others with more patience, it allows time to repair and provide the much needed maintenance to their rods and reels. For the first time in several years, our beautiful Gulf Coast looked like a "winter wonderland" as South Mississippians woke up on Saturday morning, March 13, 1993 to a couple of inches of snow and blistering winds gusting up to 50 miles per hour out of the North. St. Patrick Parades were canceled, outdoor tourist attractions were empty, most visiting "snowbirds" stayed in their hotel rooms until well past noon and the fishermen were back to repairing and fixing up their tackle.

It was actually a short, mild winter with only a few really bad days, even though the winds kept the seas too rough for the average recreational fishing boat. The bank and bridge fishing was typically slow, the inshore Trout fishing was slightly below average with the island fishing not too much better, but the offshore bottom fishing was generally excellent until the middle of March when the commercial season opened for red snapper. There continued to be plenty of small red snapper, however, the large snapper just disappeared after the 16th of March. This produced good news and bad news to the coast. The good news was that beautiful fresh red snapper would once again appear on the counters of our seafood markets. The bad news was that the multiple hook and long lines of the commercial boats drastically reduced the size of the recreational catch. So goes the life of the recreational fishermen and the commercial fishermen, each having a turn at marine resources of the Gulf of Mexico. Both having regulations and limitations on their catch. I'm confident however, that most off shore recreational fishermen did boat some great snapper catches. During a 60-90 day period in mid-winter, I was fortunate enough to get out snapper fishing a dozen or more times with fish'n buddies Ray Lanez, Grady Cook, Marty Wilson, Patrick Peterson, and John Lambeth to mention a few, and no matter who I went with, we never failed to come home with our limit or a large cooler full, which ever happened first. On one trip, with just four of us on board, allowing a legal limit of 28 snapper, we headed home early in the afternoon with just 22 beautiful fish and enough ice on top of a 178qt. cooler to get the lid closed. The larger fish weighed 16 to 24 pounds and none were smaller than 16 inches. On several trips, we lost large fish that either tore loose, broke the line or just cut the line on the rig. Most of which we never were able to turn on the initial run. On one trip, just southeast of where six of us had limited out the day before, we ran into some real heavy hitters. At first, I thought I was hung up on the bottom. Then it felt like I had hooked a big sting Ray that didn't want to come up off the bottom. But, then I remembered that I was up about 10 feet off of the bottom. Well, about that time, "Mr. Whatever It was", just decided that he wanted to go back to the rig. I put up a little struggle, however with the drag set as tight as I dared, and the deep sea rod bent in a hard "C" shape, I still was not able to keep him out of the rigs, so I tightened down the drag one more turn and put some back into it. Suddenly the line went slack and it was time all over. Within minutes, John Lambeth let out a grunt and viciously set the hook only to have the pole nearly jerked out of his hands. Once again, it appeared to be a one-sided fight as the fish gained the security of the rig and cut the line. Next, it was my son Marty's turn, and when he lost his fish, he was not pleased at all. In the course of about 30 minutes, we lost five fish of unknown species, had a legal size snapper nearly bitten in half as it was reeled in and caught three snapper in the 16 to 18 pound class. Sound like the same old "one that got away" story? Well, it's my story and I'm gonna stick with it!!

It did appear that more lemon fish (Cobia) were reported being caught by local recreational fishermen from November through March than in past years. December and January were exceptional months for both snapper and lemon fisherman. As long as the water temperature was about 70 degrees and above, excellent catches were reported from as deep as 240 feet all the up to just below the surface. On one three day trip, over two dozen legal size lemon and another half-dozen undersized were hooked and released and we still brought home the legal creel limit of 8 weighing 42 to 60 pounds, all caught at a depth of over 200 feet near rigs located about 70 miles off shore. On several other trips, small lemon were sighted around the boat, all appearing to be in a feeding frenzy, making it difficult to keep from hooking one while fishing for snapper. My friend, Jim Franks, who has become a renown Cobia authority, has concluded that even though the Cobia are normally regarded as migratory, some Cobia become homesteaders and remain in familiar waters throughout the year. I can remember when it was newsworthy to have caught the first Cobia of the year in the early spring, while now it is not uncommon to hear reports of lemon being caught at any time of the year. Granted, most are caught up to 50 miles off shore until the waters warm up on the bars around the barrier islands and the shallow rigs. For the ardent saltwater recreational sports fisherman, the month of March meant that another fishing season was just around the corner and their thoughts center around the annual question, "Will fish'n this year be better than last?" However, some other questions will come to mind. "Will the changes in the State Fish and Game Department officials help our BMR folks here on the coast?" "Will more moneys be made available for marine resource enforcement and marine research?" Will our coast fishermen, both commercial and recreational, be listened to in Jackson, regarding the desired laws, regulations and conservation?" "Are things really GETT'N BETTER? or does it just seem like we're catch'n bigger and better fish? I'm hoping that things are truly GETT'N BETTER not only right here on the Mississippi Gulf Coast, but throughout our entire Gulf of Mexico . . . How about you??

SOME DAYS IT'S CHICKEN,
SOME DAYS IT'S FEATHERS,
SOME DAYS IT'S JUST
PLAIN CHICKEN ____!

Anyone that has ever gone fish'n with my 'ol salty look'n fish'n buddy, Grady Cook, has bound to have heard him utter one of his countless personal evaluations of the current situation before, during or after a fishing trip. One of his quips that seems to cover about any fishing trip I have ever been on goes like this; "Some days it's Chicken, Some days it's Feathers, and Some days it's just plain Chicken ____!!!" Well Folks, I can truthfully say that I have been on both ends of that spectrum and any fisherman that tells you that they have not been there is either not a avid fisherman or is the proverbial fisherman that everyone accuses of being the teller of tall tales. Even Fred Deegen and John Lambeth will confess to you that, while fishing is the art of casting, trolling, jigging or spinning, while freezing, sweating, swatting, repairing and swearing, there are days that end up with just being a bad boat ride.

The top of the spectrum starts out with an absolutely, fantastic beautiful sunrise, with the seas near calm and a rare beautiful blue-green color well inside the barrier islands. The water turns into a rich deep blue with crystal tops on the wake behind our boat as we head southeast on the other side of the islands. Well before we reached the first oilrigs we sighted birds working bait fish in every direction we looked. Small schools of mackerel, Bonito and blue runners could be seen slapping the water as they too fed on the thousands of small bait fish. Wow! What a day this looked like it was going to be, and what a day it was. Throughout the morning, regardless of rather we were trolling or bottom fishing, we caught fish. We started to cull out our catch by mid morning, just to keep from limiting out before noon. Lemon fish, red snapper, grouper and King

Mackerel nearly filled our two 178 qt. coolers and our biggest fear was having to give up the ice cold beer space for another big fish before heading for home. But, needless to say, things never got quite that bad, (Or should I say good?) as we all enjoyed a cool one on the way back to port. The air was filled with everyone talking at once, reminiscing to anyone that would listen, about the one that couldn't be turned, or the prize catch of the day. Yes, it had been a super day. But the gravy came when we tied up at the dock and the local folks and tourists all come to take a peek at our catch. Tired, sun burnt arms held up their prize catch and chests were proudly expanded as the cameras clicked away. Now that day we got the whole chicken!!!

Now, on 90 percent of the other trips and lets call this the middle of the spectrum, the morning starts out pretty nice with the sun trying to peek through the clouds on the eastern horizon. The water doesn't start to change from brownish-green to a fairly clear blue-green color until several miles on the other side of the islands. Seems like it takes longer than normal to get to the rigs and little or no activity is seen on the surface. As we approach the rigs, we noted that all our favorite rigs were covered by other boats. So, we start trolling around from rig to rig, hoping to pick up something as we search for a good rig to fish. We do manage to pick up a small king or two, but the action is really slow. We end up fishing hard all day and as normal, head home with a respectable catch, but certainly nothing to really brag about. Kinda gives you the feeling that maybe you just got the feathers and not the whole chicken. Know what I mean? But, 'ja know what? Maybe we are a little bit spoiled, 'cause I know lots of folks that I have taken fishing and felt it was one of those feathers days with just enough fish to stink up the skillet good, but they were happy. Some even told me that it was more fish than they had ever caught on one trip. So, maybe, feathers ain't too bad.

But, the very worse end of the spectrum is when you have waited weekend after weekend for the weather to clear and you know your just gonna die with cabin fever, and along comes a marginal weather break. You get up that morning to some real "iffy" weather reports and yet it looks like it might be a great day. So, you load up and head down to the launching ramp, determined to be as optimistic as possible. Although the flag at the small craft harbor is not indicating much wind, you soon find out that small craft warnings are forecasted for later in the morning. But, the residual effects from two weeks of cabin fever cloud your better judgment, and you all agree to go for it. Off we go, into a 5 to 10 kt. wind blowing a slight drizzle just enough to be uncomfortable. But, that's just the beginning. The seas don't appear to get any worse as you head southeast off the tip of the barrier island, but you note that the water color isn't getting any better either. The brownish water gradually turns to a blue greenish color somewhere about an hour out, but the seas appear to be increasing. The boat seems to be handling well and the rest of the party on board, appear ok, so we press on.

About the time the rigs are in sight several things are happening. The seas are noticeably rougher and one engine just doesn't seem to be running right. But, with the rigs so close, and your better judgment still a little clouded, you press on and with amazingly little difficulty, we were soon secured to the rig. But things start happening then. First, someone lost the chum sack overboard while they were trying to secure it at the back of the boat. The fresh bait and cigar minnows that we had bought that morning are not nearly so fresh, and two of our fishing buddies suddenly don't feel so good and start their own chumming. You soon learn that the only place that you could tie up, due to the wind, is also directly over some pipe and cable. So after losing several hooks and sinkers, we decided to move on to another rig. This time, it was a little more difficult to get tied up and we should have just started for home then and there. But we didn't. We just kept thinking it would get better. But it didn't.

By noon, there were still no eat'n fish in the cooler and everyone was silently thinking that they should have stayed home in bed with Ma Ma, especially those that were still chumming every so often. Finally, they broke the silence and between moans and groans, they coaxed us to give up and head for homeport. So, with a half sick engine, two full sick fishermen and an empty ice chest, except for nearly two cases of beer that were almost forgotten, we started the long trip home. As we tied up at the dock, we almost all got sick for we couldn't help but notice the beautiful catch that was proudly displayed on the very next dock. Adding insult to injury, the captain of the other boat spoke in a non-chalant way, "Hi there! How'd ya'll do? Man we really got the whole chicken today!!" Little did he know that our day had really been just plain chicken ____!!!!!!! So now you know what ol Grady means when he says, "Some days it's Chicken, Some days it's Feathers and Some days it's just plain Chicken ____!!!

GULF WINTER WATERLAND

Every morning that I plan to go fishing, the very first thing that I do is check the weather. Spring, Summer, Fall or Winter. It makes no difference what time of year, because the weather is the major determining factor on go or no-go days. Usually during the summer months I can plan for a fishing trip a couple of days in advance. Spring and Fall can and does produce some unpredictable weather at times, but the guess'n really gets tough during the winter months and so far, this winter has been no exception. Only on rare occasions could we plan an off-shore fishing trip over 48 hours in advance. Either the weather was forecasted to be horrible and so we sat at home and watched a beautiful day from dawn till dark because a forecasted cold front stalled out and didn't make it to the coast. Or, what was forecasted to be a pleasant, fair-weather day on the water, turns into a cold, rainy and windy day. Either way it seems like ya' end up loosing, especially if its on a weekend or holiday.

Well, even with the adverse weather conditions encountered, the good days that we outguessed the forecast were usually very productive. And, the beautiful, crisp, Gulf Winter Waterland was breathtaking and exhilarating during the early morning sunrise. The days that we were able to reach our chosen destination became fewer and fewer as the new year approached, however it seemed like the "catch'n" got better each trip. Early in the quarter, trips to the sunken ships and rubble or the rigs always produced red snapper limits, a King Mackerel or two and maybe even a lemon fish. Various half-day trips to the Ship Island rock pile or the Gulfport ship channel totem pole usually produce an abundance of big old yellow-mouthed White Trout, some Ground Mullet and even a few Speckled Trout, if the gill-netters had not beat you to them.

One sunny morning in early November, my long time fishing friend, Grady Cook and I were on our way to the Getty Rigs and we were forced back due to increasing seas. Disappointed but not beaten, we headed for shelter inside the barrier islands. Hoping there might still be some fish around the rock pile, we were soon anchored and rigging our light tackle for a little bottom fishing. We had some cigar minnows and some old frozen bait, but we knew that all we needed to do was catch just one little ol` White Trout and we were in business. Well, I chipped off a hunk of rotten old purple squid and cast as far out to the outer edge of the rock pile as I could. The bait barely touched the bottom when, POW!! I liked to got the rod jerked out of my hand. Once I produced my nice big ol` yeller mouthed White Trout over the side of the boat, Grady immediately went to squid. Well, no matter how bad and how rotten that squid was, we sat there and literally filled a cooler full of well over-a-pound size White Trout. Noticing that the seas were still increasing with the wind now coming around the end of the island, we pulled anchor and headed for da` house. Well, fresh "just been caught" White Trout are just about as good a eat'n as you could want, so you can bet what we had for supper that night.

Not too much later that month, the weather not only was forecasted to be pretty good, but it was good and once again, Grady and I headed for the "Gettys". Even though the seas were a little choppy on the way out we still made pretty good headway and were tied up to a rig and fish'n in less than 2 hours from leaving the Biloxi Harbor. Now this is one trip that "fo sure" could be called a catch'n trip as well as a fish'n trip, cause we did catch some fish. It was one of those days that someone else always tells you about. Nearly every time you dropped your hook over the side you caught a fish and every time you got a bite. We not only limited out with some fine Red Snapper in the 15 to 20 inch class, but we caught Bluefish, Trigger Fish, grouper, Hardtails and Redfish. Well the grouper were much too small, the Redfish could not be kept in federal waters, and the Hardtail and Trigger were throw backs, but the variety presented a real challenge to be able to name the fish right after you hooked it. The water was crystal clear and you could see your catch coming up from about 20 feet down. We must have caught and released over two dozen Redfish, all between 24 to 30 inches. I fully believe that they all survived. For the first time in all the years that I have fished with Grady, I really think that he got his fill of catching fish that day, for a mid-point in the afternoon, he laid down his rod, sat down and advised that he was plum tuckered out and needed a rest. Since it was nearly 3 p.m. in the afternoon anyway, we just called it a day and headed home.

I guess the trip that was the most memorable however, was late in November when Jim Franks and I went on another great "catching trip" with John Lambeth on the "Hot Story". Exactly one year ago, Ray Lenaz, Jimmy Lenaz, John and I had caught our limit of Lemonfish in over 200 feet around some oil rigs nearly 70 miles off-shore and that's where we were heading. This was going to be some kind of a "scientific" trip for Jim Franks who is known by many as the "Lemonfish guru" for his tireless research study of the much sought after Cobia. We needed to know if the brown beauties were there in this deep water like they were this time last year. Well, the day started real early and as we loaded the boat with enough fishing gear, bait and nourishment for 10 fishermen, we marveled at the beautiful full moon overhead, which made it almost like daylight in the dimly lit harbor. By the time we got underway and were in a stones throw of Ship Island, the moon was about to be replaced by a beautiful orange glow that was just starting to show on the eastern horizon. What a beautiful and magnificent sunrise we witnessed as we headed southeast, for our destination. Things warmed up considerably, with the giant ball of fire doing a super job as it climbed higher in the sky. By the time we tied up to the rig, we had all shed an outer layer of clothes and were hot to fish. Jim was ready and quickly dropped his baited hook into the water before John or I even got baited, however I must tell you that ol' Tricky Dick drew first blood. Even though it was a keeper Snapper, it was not quite what we were looking for just yet and I quickly released it to go find big mama. About this time Jim's bait hit the bottom and he let out a loud grunt. His rod bent into the familiar "C" shape as he set the hook hard. John let out a loud, "Whoot, There it is!!" and we frantically started to reel in our lines to keep from tangling with Jim's. But, not quite quick enough, as Jim's fish had headed for the rig and crossed my line. So, Jim and I played his fish like we both had one on with Jim in command. Finally, after much concern over the tangled lines, we got our first glimpse of his fighter and we all cried out in unison, "Lemon"!!

As Jim continued to play his fish, John and I worked on carefully untangling the lines each time there was a slight break in the fight. As soon as the lines were worked free, John grabbed the long handled gaff and at just the right time, made one expert move on the Cobia. In that one smooth motion, the fish was gaffed, hauled over the side and into the waiting open fish box. The "Lemonfish man" had caught the very fish we had come all this way to get. With the lid on the fish box tightly closed, and the gaff stowed, a round of hard hitting "high 5's" celebrated the catch. Jim then quietly sat down for a well, deserved rest. Anyone that has ever fought a fish that weighs over 40 pounds all the way to the surface from over 200 feet deep knows exactly how tired and drained Jim felt at that minute, for just a minute or two before, he had been on pure adrenalin.

As John and I smiled and looked at each other, we both knew that if we never caught another fish all day, the trip was already a success. Jim Franks had done did it!! But there's more. For the next hour we caught Bluefish, Trigger Fish and Snapper consistently until suddenly, I hooked into something that flat stopped me from reeling for a minute. As I lifted the rod tip high and started to pump the rod, I felt a strong downward drive in response. Again I pumped the rod to move the mass upward and it was just as determined to stay down there. This went on until I had the fish about half way up to the surface and then things got better. I had guessed from the start what it was and this almost confirmed it, so I was not disappointed when a big ol' 18 pound Grouper came into view. Within minutes of my Grouper being iced down in the fish box, Jim Franks let out one of his familiar grunts as he made a powerful upward swing with his rod only to be stopped about half-way through the arc as the big fish felt the hook. Down went the rod tip and another 20 feet of line zipped through the rod guides. As John and I both frantically reeled in our lines, we both agreed that Jim had hooked into another Lemon. Twelve minutes later, John made another great gaff job and now the Lemonfish guru had two of his favorite fish in the box. Well, the rest of the day would have been rather anti-climatic if John had not hooked into the biggest snapper of the day. A big ol' 20 pounder. At first, we all thought that he had himself a nice Lemon, but as the fight progressed, we agreed that it was fighting different than the Lemon that Jim had caught. So, as the dark, red-orange beauty came into view, we were really not too surprised. Not too longer after that we cut loose from the rig and started the trip home. The seas were still a little choppy as we headed toward the Gulfport Harbor, but the closer that we got to the barrier islands, the smoother the water became. By the time that we passed abeam of the Chandeleur lighthouse, the shadows had lengthened, the sun was making it's dazzling bright disappearance in the west and the smiles on all of our faces were still lingering. We passed the western tip of Ship Island just as the moon was starting its red glow on the horizon. Another unbelievable sight, as it made it's bright appearance into the clear black sky and turned into a beautiful white ball with a shimmering crystal reflection across the now calm waters of the Gulf. We had seen the moon go down, the sun come up and then set; the moon rise again and there are no words to describe the beauty of it all. Winters are not all that bad, as we had just experienced a beautiful day on the Gulf Winter Wonderland.

BERTHA—A BIRD AND A STORM

This is about another one of those crazy trips where maybe a little better judgment on—"Go or no Go" might have saved a few gray hairs. The forecast for the weekend was really not the best, as a possible tropical depression was trying to form off the Louisiana coast, but appeared to be slow in developing, so we said, "Heck with it, what's a little rough water"? And off we went, on another great trip to the rigs down South.

After a rather quick preparation and loading of the necessary tackle and basic survival stuff, (like beer, peanut and jelly sandwiches, some cold chicken, and tootsie lollypops we stopped and got some fresh bait, a dozen Croakers and we were on our way. It didn't take long to launch and depart the Biloxi Harbor and upon clearing the "no wake area, the powerful twin Mercury Optimax outboards roared to life and the 26 Foot Mako, ("MY REEL MISTRESS") responded accordingly. We had even filed an overnight float plan with the BMR. Oh yes, Terry Stewart, Steve Stewart, George Junkert, Steve Wilson and yours truly were on board. (The sixth member of our fishing team, poor Marty Wilson was just too busy painting murals at the, soon to open, "COPA".) We did however, have an additional passenger on board we called, "Birdie". You see Birdie was Steve Wilson's "pet" bird that he hand feeds daily and has been on several prior, fishing trips.

Well, as we passed through Dog Key Pass at Horn Island, we quickly noted that our trip to the deep rigs could be a slow, bumpy ride, as white caps were rolling across the bar. But, much to our surprise, as we traveled further South, the height of the seas gradually decreased and around three in the afternoon, we arrived at the Sulphur Rigs, located nearly 80 miles South of Biloxi. Steve Wilson quickly secured our shepherd hook to one of the rigs and we all got ready to fish. We had only been there a few minutes and Terry put a real nice Grouper in the box! By Sunset, we also had several nice Red Snapper, another smaller Grouper, and about a dozen 2 to 3 pound White Trout. Since this was not the rig that we had planned on spending the night, about an hour before sunset, we

147

cranked up the engines and headed East to the Horseshoe Rigs. The seas had picked up a little bit, due to some large thunderstorms to the East Northeast.

The Sun was just trying to set as we reached the "Horseshoes" and hooked up to one of our favorite rigs located in a depth of about 220 to 225 feet. Since our back up rigs were already and ready to fish for Amberjack, it only took seconds for everyone to wet a line. Within minutes, we landed our first Amberjack and before the Sun had set, we had landed our one fish limit. Wow! Spirits peaked! And the great part was that each of us caught one. All fish were caught while jigging with a diamond jig at about the 150 foot depth. We then rigged our lines with about a 3 to 4 foot steel leader and a 5.0 or 7.0 stainless steel "J" hook with at least an 8-ounce lead weight. (This was several years before the circle hook was required in federal waters.) Steve Wilson was the only one that was not back to fishing, as he was busy feeding "Birdie" his evening meal.

As one of the thunderstorms appeared to be slowly heading in our direction, Terry and his son, Steve stopped fishing long enough to spread a large tarp, tied from the bow to the top of the T-Top over the center console, in case of a typical, sudden down pour. Periodically, we each stopped fishing long enough to suck down a beer and munch on a snack or sandwich. We continued fishing, telling jokes and consuming a beer now and then, (mostly now) until shortly after midnight, using just the light shinning down from the rig. The fish had almost stopped biting, but we had caught several nice fish. Steve Wilson had caught a large eel that we thought to be a Conger Eel and later proved to be a state record. Steve and I both caught a couple of rather rare Rock Hine Groupers. Steve's was the largest and later was determined to be another state record. Two state records on one trip!! Terry, Steve Stewart and George had each caught some nice Red Snapper and were still telling jokes, but slowing down as the evening moved to early morning. So we kinda settled down, taking periodic cat-naps when a large thunderstorm hit us with some 6 to7 foot swells that were coming through the rig. It became somewhat uncomfortable in minutes. As the storm seemed to intensify, we all huddled under the t-top and then moved up under the canvas to stay out of the wind and rain. We eventually got used to the rock and rolling and started to doze off. Suddenly, a giant wave broke over the bow, dumping over a foot of water over all the "dozing" fishermen and scared the heck out of everyone. We quickly got the bilge pumps going and soon had a relatively dry hull again within minutes the storm passed through and after checking our lines, we dozed off again.

We were all up at the crack of dawn. There were major thunderstorms all around the area, dumping serious rain. It was time to head for home. As we departed the rig, it appeared that we could quarter into the wind and seas and ride the 7 to 8 foot swells up and over each wave. We tried repeatedly to raise some one on the radio, including CH 16, to get a weather report, but no one replied. As a result, we had no idea that our little tropical depression had turned into a tropical storm, which later developed into Hurricane Bertha. Soon we were all soaked and starting to shiver in the cooler wind. Even "Birdie" was not looking too good and Steve put one of his shirts over the cage. As we plugged along, we encountered 10 to 12 foot swells with a chop on top that would come tumbling over the bow and sometimes even swing along the side of the aft section, literally filling the back of the boat with water. The bilge pumps were barely keeping up. Things were not looking good. About that time, Steve Wilson muttered, something about "The Perfect Storm", which brought about a few nervous laughs. We continued to grind along, fighting each wave and when we noticed that the bilge pumps were not keeping up, we even had someone bailing the back end with a bucket. The wind was blowing freezing rain and someone got the idea of using our sleeping bags like a wet-suit to brake the wind and it worked. Steve Wilson and I took turns at the wheel while others made sure that the water that was coming over the bow was not going to swamp us. After what seemed like hours of torrential rain and mountainous waves, we passed through the shallow rigs South of Chandeleur. As we approached the cut just to the South of Monkey Bayou, we made our dash across the bar and headed inside the island seeking some relief from the howling wind and raging seas. However, the rain began to come down even worse as the never ending wind and rain continued to reduce the visibility to near zero. We had to totally rely on our GPS and just as we were approaching Schooner Harbor, the rain let up and we could see the island. Someone spotted a little light over toward shore and we headed toward it. At first, it looked like a Snapper boat or some kind of barge, then I recognized that it was the "Pelican" houseboat. (A fishing barge where fishermen can stay and are provided a boat, motor and guide to fish all around the island.) Looking to the South, I spotted the red buoy that marked the entrance to the channel that leads into the "Pelican". As we maneuvered the channel and approached the houseboat, several people were out on the front porch waving at us. We received a genuine warm welcome as we boarded the houseboat. I recognized some of the faces and a couple of names as they introduced themselves one by one. Once the boat was secured and we were inside, we were immediately provided dry towels and something warm to drink. With that, they also offered dry clothes and insisted that we stay the night or as long as needed till the storm passed. The remainder of the evening was just fantastic. Even "Birdie" perked up and talked to Steve as he dried his feathers and fed him.

Following a warm shower, dry clothes and a really great supper prepared by "Sonny" Ty Cox, a Biloxi native, and everything was just great. We did contribute a couple of our big Snapper to the feast, which Ty prepared to perfection. Ty is the "Pelican" first mate, cook, guide and B. S. Artist. We really begin to relax as we watched the weather on TV. Yes, they even had TV. And we learned that "BERTHA" was the name of the storm. The wind and rain was still howling outside as we chatted and enjoyed ourselves with our new friends. Brad New, was also a guide and one of the crew. (He was a former fishing partner with my son, Marty Wilson during the famous annual Florida "Crab Crunch") Others on board were: Dr. Shea Penland, PHD, a professor of Geology at UNO; Carol Franze, a research associate also at UNO and Paul Conner, an aerial photo biological researcher. Really a great group of folks that offered their hospitality and made us feel very comfortable. (I would also mention that, the "Pelican" was owned by Captain Mark Stebly of Ocean Springs, Ms.)

Early the next morning, the sun was peaking through the clouds and it appeared that the storm had moved on. After a great breakfast, we loaded up the boat and said our goodbyes. When asked how much our "bill" was, the reply was, "Not a dime, we were happy to be able to help". Brad asked if the bird had a real name and Steve replied, "Nope, just "Birdie". Brad then suggested that we might want to rename it "BERTHA" as a reminder of the trip. We all agreed and with that we departed. The trip back to Biloxi was uneventful and by noon, we entered the Biloxi Harbor and soon had "MY REEL MISTRESS" on the trailer. And as we rolled down the road, it was a tired but happy crew that had made it home from a storm and with a bird named "BERTHA"!

COBIA SECOND MIGRATION

Most Gulf Coast saltwater fishermen are quite familiar with the spring migration of the much respected and sought after Cobia and each year look forward to their annual arrival with great anticipation. Cobia, which are also commonly known as "Lemonfish" in Alabama, Mississippi and Louisiana, migrate from the Florida Keys early each spring, to the north along the Florida Panhandle. As they run along the front beaches of Panama City, Destin and Pensacola, the art of precision "sight casting" is the most productive technique used, as thousands of Cobia anglers greet them with tantalizing jigs, live eels, small live Finfish and various types of colorful artificial lures.

In a matter of weeks, the migrating Cobia have moved on west, past Mobile Bay, bouncing to the outside of the "Barrier Islands", which includes Dauphin, Petit Bois, Horn, Ship (East and West), and even Cat Island. Many of these hungry fish continue to fall pray to more Cobia fishermen that anchor on the edge of many sand bars along the way. They entice the feeding brown beauties to their baited hooks by establishing a long, rich "chum-line", consisting of ground up fish mixed with fish oil and other favorite smelly attractions. Normally, live "Hardhead" Catfish, live Eels and small line Finfish are again offered as bait and may be presented under a float or balloon, free lined or just laying on the bottom under the chum stream. Horn Island bar in the Mississippi sound and the various bars off the North end of Chandeleur Island are two favorite areas during the spring. As the water temperature of the Mississippi Sound and the "Gulf" increase each day in late spring, the Cobia move on into a little deeper, cooler water, looking for a comfort zone with both food and structure.

The migration continues on down Chandeleur Island. The fish spread out into the deeper water and the many underwater structures of the Gulf, such as the hundreds of oilrigs. Another favorite hide out is under the many large shrimp boats that lay at anchor during day, sorting their catch and cleaning their nets and decks. Here, however they must compete for the unwanted "by-catch" being washed overboard, with other hungry predators, such as the feisty Jack

Cravelle, Bonnito, and various types of Sharks. The annual migration continues on through the summer and a few different techniques are now used to entice the Cobia to take the bait. Keep in mind that the surviving Cobia are a lot smarter now, as along the way, they have seen a lot of different baits and evaded a lot of fishermen. But, Cobia have a common fatal trait. They are very curious and even when not in the feeding mood while cruising the bottom, they will become curious and interested in a jerking bait or the sound of something near the surface and will rise to see what is making the commotion. Revving up the boat motor will sometimes bring up as many as a half dozen or more curious Cobia. Even just beating on the water with paddle or fishing rod has worked as it may sound like feeding frenzy. When Cobia are spotted, jigs, live Eels or live Catfish are quickly offered and many times a small or medium sized Finfish may be hooked and left in the water to splash and flip around, again simulating a feeding frenzy and sometimes attracting other Cobia in the area. The presentation is many time a "give and take" technique, as when they see the bait, you take it away simulating a fleeing meal, and they will attack. As they take the bait, it is wise to let them run a little prior to setting the hook, yet not so long as to let them have time to spit it out. But, that comes with experience and even then they may feel the hook and release early. As the Cobia continue from structure to structure, rig to rig, making their counterclockwise migration, summer drifts into fall, and now they are entering into a "second migration".

There is a noticeable change, as the majority of the fish move through the shallow rigs and feed as the water starts to cool more and more. Most are moving south-southeast and some are starting their migration back to the "Keys". Normally by late October, groups of Cobia become less plentiful and by the time the water temperature is in the low 60's in late November, there are but a few stragglers sighted near the surface. (This year has been somewhat of an exception due to the hurricanes and late fall warmer temperatures. Following "Katrina", literally hundreds of Cobia was sighted at the shallow rigs to the south of Chandeleur in the late months of fall.)

But, the Cobia story does not end there. During the winter months, many Cobia stories may be heard around the "fish camps", regarding the late fall "bite". It is important to know that marine biologists have stated that though it is unusual to catch Cobia as late as December, they have been caught in deep water all winter long. Jim Franks, a well respected leader in a Gulf-wide Cobia research study, conducted by the Mississippi Gulf Coast Marine Research laboratory in Ocean

Springs, has always theorized that some Cobia do not migrate to the Keys. He even went a step further and organized a fishing trip in, December, 1992, to personally see if some could be located. It just happens that this writer was on board that day along with former Sun Herald outdoors editor John Lambeth. Franks is known as the Cobia "guru" throughout the whole Gulf of Mexico as he has studied them for many years. He even surpassed himself, while on this 1992 trip, when he personally caught four of the elusive brownies in depths of nearly 200 feet. The fish all weighed between 30 to 45 pounds and were found to be in excellent condition. He also found that the water temperature at that depth was an amazing 72 degrees (F) and he theorized that the fish had located a comfortable temperature range and had enough food available to remain through the winter months. Several other Cobia catches have also been reported during the cold winter months since then. However, Franks did acknowledge that the majority of the Cobia do move on with their "second migration", in quest of returning to the warm waters of the lower Gulf and the "Keys". Then once again they start their early spring migration to the north. And so, this completes the first and second migration of the great brown Cobia, as it moves throughout the beautiful Gulf of Mexico, attracting thousands of fishing enthusiasts.

DO YOU INTEND T0 EAT THIS FISH, SON?

How well I recall some of the fondest memories of my early Boy hood days, fishing with my Father and Uncle Frank, on the many lakes in Northern Indiana. I remember the thrill and nervous excitement I felt as I pitted my small, three year old body against the magnificent strength and powerful downward pull of my first feisty Blue Gill. The enormous 12 foot long "Cinderella" cane pole I was now hanging on to for dear life, seemed to bend double. I feared that that the thin black fishing line would break any moment. My shrill cries for my Father to help me seemed to fall on deaf ears. Finally, with my heart pounding, and my arms exhausted. I felt a sudden wave of relief and pride, as my prize lay flopping on the bottom of the boat. My joy was short lived, however, as my Father picked up my fish and as he removed the hook, ask me a question that I shall never forget. "Do you intend to eat this fish, Son? If not, we need to hurry and release it so it will live."

I was shocked and felt betrayed. How could he? "No! No! Don't! Please don't Daddy!" I exclaimed. "I mean, Yes! Yes! We'll eat it!" I shouted, as tears filled my eyes. With mixed emotions, I was so proud that my first fish was considered big enough to eat. Yet, I was near panic that my Father was going to release it anyway. But, he gently patted my shoulder and cheerfully said, "O.K. Son, but we need to catch a few more if we plan to make a meal for the whole family." I sighed in relief, as he placed what seemed to me, to be the worlds' biggest "six-inch" blue gill into the cooler.

As I looked back in later years, I knew that this was my first lesson, in "catch and release". If you aren't going to eat it, put it back! And, that was over 75 years ago. How time flies. I still get all excited while fishing with light tackle and I hook up with a big old Lemon, King, Redfish, Jack, Dolphin, Wahoo, Tuna, Black Drum or even a hefty Blacktip Shark. But, I get even more of a thrill watching any of my boys and Grandchildren fighting a scrappy Speckled

159

Trout, or a hard fighting Redfish, or even a hefty Sheepshead. Hopefully, I will get to fish with all my Grandchildren often, and as the years go by, they too will always remember, "DO YOU INTEND TO EAT THIS FISH, SON? IF NOT, WE NEED TO HURRY AND RELEASE IT SO IT WILL LIVE."

"LIFE IS SHORT—FISH HARD"
(QUOTE—MARTY WILSON)

As Fall of 2011 moved into the early Winter months, the larger Speckled Trout and Redfish made their annual inshore appearance. The Bays and Rivers were producing respectable catches nearly everywhere. Live bait was readily available. Even as the first cold North wind started to penetrate the Gulf Coast, good catches continued to be reported. However, in late December and the first week of 2012, things begin to change. More Rat-Reds and small Black Drum were being reported, and fewer large Specks. Sheepshead were becoming a common catch, especially around the bridges and piers.

Winter!!! Yep! Santa's been here and gone. The beautiful Christmas music and celebration of our dear Jesus' birthday is still ringing in our ears, as the chilly northwest winds make early morning fishing less attractive. By mid-January, the evening and early morning temperatures dropped into the 20's and fewer and fewer of the large Specks were reported. My oldest son, Steve, had been very successful during the previous months and on several occasions had proudly displayed his catch of Specks in the 3 to 5 pound class. On a couple of trips, I accompanied him and shared the thrill of catching several of the beautiful large Specks and Redfish on light tackle. However, as early as the day before New Years Eve, things begin to change drastically. The early morning tides were very low as we dropped anchor at one of our favorite fishing locations. The north wind continued to hold out the incoming tide until well into the afternoon. Winter was really here. As the sun begin to hide behind the low forming clouds in the West, we pulled anchor and headed for the dock, but this time our cooler was nearly full of above average Sheepshead and 5 to 7 pound Black Drum. Not one Speck was caught all day! And even though we caught a lot of Rat Reds, not one was big enough to keep.

Upon arrival at the D'Iberville boat launch, located under the I-I0 Bridge, we talked to a couple of officers with the Mississippi Marine Law Enforcement, and were not too surprised to learn that they had only seen 5 Specks all day as they checked other fishing boats. Well, that did not make us feel too much better, however, having fished together for well over 50 years, we were both able to just smile, count our blessings, thank the two guardians of our Mississippi Marine life and start thinking about what a great fish dinner we were about to have with what we had caught. With lots of cold days and nights still ahead before the Spring winds begin to warm up the waters let us not forget, as my youngest son, Marty often says, "LIFE IS SHORT—FISH HARD! !"

RELEASE THE BIG SOWS

Wind, wind and more wind! This Spring, week after week, strong winds continued long after March and discouraged even the most dedicated saltwater fishermen from venturing into open waters. However, some strong cases of "cabin fever" did force a few to go fight the elements and participate in their 2nd favorite sport. But, finally, as the days get longer and Spring, now racing towards Summer, the early morning winds are lighter and skies are sunny all day.

One such morning in mid May, I was able to time my plans so as to hit a day when winds are to be light and sky was deep blue. Originally, I had planned on taking my little 19-foot open fisherman, but while discussing our fishing trip with one of my regular fishing buddies, Michael Peterson, he suggested that we take his boat as he needs to use it and enjoys every minute that he can spend on it. '"DONE!" I quickly replied. Michael was born and raised in Biloxi; retired Air Force, (Three star General) and has chosen fishing over the game of golf. He is an ardent fisherman and a pleasure to fish with.

At 6AM sharp, "Mike" was parked in front of my house and upon quickly loading my gear, we headed to the D'Iberville Boat Launch, located under the I-110 bridge. Our original plan was to grab some live bait from the closest bait shop and check out the fishing reefs located in the Mississippi Sound, however following a rather bumpy ride out to FH-9/11, we felt it best not to go any further and just keep an eye on the winds. After a couple of hours of catching small White Trout, Croaker, pin fish and more that we wanted, hard-head catfish, we headed back towards shore to the "White House" reef using the GPS for most direct route. Once again, however, it was small White Trout, Croaker, and hard head catfish. But, we did a have little excitement when mike hooked into the first of several large gaff top catfish. After over a half an hour of this, I became bored and prior to suggesting that we move, I put on a little larger circle hook and baited my largest Trout rig with a 3-inch Croaker and threw it out to let it soak for a while. Within 5 minutes the rod bent double and the drag begin to sing my song. I didn't even have to yell, "Fish On!". Mike had already reeled in his line, grabbed the landing net and was standing ready on my side of the boat.

During the next 5 or 6 minutes it was a give and take battle, as the still unknown bottom fish would peal off 15 to 20 yards each time before I could turn him back toward the boat. However, finally the tail (tell) sign, revealing a beautiful gold color on the surface, resulted in our unified cry "REDFISH!" Not wanting to push my luck using 17 pound test line, I played the beauty a little longer than I normally would, but soon landed the beautiful 30 plus pound sow. After carefully extracting the circle hook from the corner of her mouth, and a quick picture, we released the beauty, knowing that she would soon produce over 50,000 eggs and hopefully make it possible for the next generation to enjoy the same thrill.

But, the day was not over. Mike quickly rigged his gear and within minutes was hooked up to what we believed to be another golden beauty. And to his joy, it was. After a similar courageous fight, I netted the fish and following a picture, a quick release. During the next couple of hours we caught some nice White Trout, several large Gaff Top Catfish, tons of Croaker and THREE MORE BIG SOW REDFISH!!! All were released except the biggest White Trout and two of the largest gaff top catfish save for another fishing friend of ours. Mike and I discussed the fact that even though each of the big "sows" could produce well over 50,000 eggs, only a very small percent would actually survive to hatch, make it through the juvenile and "rat-red" stage and become a magnificent adult Redfish. At this point, the rest of the trip was incidental and just a great day on the beautiful Mississippi Sound.

TEEN TAMES SHARK

The first gray light of dawn began to show in the East, as we loaded our 28 foot, "My Reel Mistress", with what seemed like tons of fishing gear, chum, bait, and coolers full of food and beverages. All this in preparation for a two day trip south to the many oil rigs, as we were entered in the Annual Ocean Springs Elk's Memorial Day Fishing Rodeo. Since our regular tournament fishing team of five was down to three this trip, consisting of Terry Stewart, my oldest son, Steve and myself, we also invited Terry's, 14 year old, son to go with us. His name was also Steve, so we called him "Little Steve" and my son, "Big Steve", even though at 14 he was almost as tall as "Big Steve". (Note: This happened 10 years ago, and Little Steve is now BIG Steve and Big Steve is now Little Steve in comparison. Kids do grow up!)

As soon as the boat was loaded, we headed for the Biloxi Small Craft Harbor and following a quick launching of the boat, stopped by Pat Kaluz's Bait and Fuel Dock for Ice and some live Croakers. Finally, we headed south! Wow! Did it feel good! With the wind in our face, with the Warm morning sun and the light sea spray, it was just the right combination, along with smooth sounding harmony of the twin 225 HP Mercury outboards producing pure music to our ears. And as we slipped by the barrier islands, then the Chandeluer Light, on past the Data Buoy, we marveled at the relatively calm seas. Our spirits were high and young Steve Stewart had a big ol' smile on his face.

Shortly after passing the Data Buoy, we came across a couple of shrimp boats drifting along as they washed down their decks from the evening catch. Large fish were working around the stern of the first boat. Terry and I jumped to the bow and began jigging four ounce feather jigs, while Steve Wilson maneuvered the boat into position behind the shrimp boat. Wham! As soon as my jig hit the water, I had a hook-up and in minutes, I horsed aboard a hefty Jack Crevalle. About that time, we noted that the fish feeding were Jacks and Bonito, so we hung around a little while, thinking that this would be great fun for Steve Stewart. Big Steve handed him a seven-foot Okuma Pursuit rod with a Okuma

CN 30L level wind reel full of 25# test braided line and said, "Ok son, it's your turn". Within seconds of making his first cast, his rod was suddenly bent over from the force of a hard-hitting Jack. Having never caught a Jack before, Steve was all at once like a young cowboy trying to bulldog his first steer. Every time he got the fish up near the boat, it made a quick turn and headed south. Finally, he tightened down the drag and brought the valiant fighter to the boat. Both the fish and angler were totally exhausted. His catch looked big enough to maybe place in the rodeo, so we chunked it into the big ice chest and headed out to deeper water.

As we moved on South, the first of the shallow water oilrigs became visible and more and more appeared for miles ahead. Wow! What a beautiful clear day. We all were just "chomp'n at the bit" to get a line wet. By the time we got to one of the deeper rigs, Steve Stewart was baited and in the water, before we were even hooked to the rig. As it turned out, the rig was loaded with big Redfish and small Red Snapper. But since we could not keep the Redfish in Federal waters and the snapper were all too small to keep, we moved on South to another rig. The next rig also produced Redfish and small Snapper, however we did hook a small Cobia, which we quickly netted, tagged and released ASAP. By this time it was past noon, so we continued on south for another hour and picked out one of our favorite rigs to spend the night in about 145 feet of water.

Much to our delight, the water surrounding the rig was teaming with "tons" of Hardtails, also called Bluerunners, great baitfish for, large Snapper, Grouper or Amberjack. The water was just beautiful!! Not quite the deep blue-green that you find further South, but it sure looked good to us as we secured the "Shepherd" hook to the corner of the rig. The first thing that we did was fish for the baitfish. After putting over a couple dozen in the live well, we baited up and set out six lines. Two were with balloons, floating some distance from the back of the boat with lively "Hardtails" hanging down about three or four feet on a large hook. Two other lines were baited with live Croakers and just "free-lined", (no weight) just behind the boat. The final two were baited with cut bait and squid and dropped to the bottom. All four rods were placed in the rod holders with drag set loose and the "clickers" on. I personally prefer this, over using the free-spool method, as even with the clicker on, a King, Wahoo, or even a Bonito can hit so swiftly, it can create a serious backlash. Next, we setup our chum line, using the famous "Chum-Churn" and then we just settled down to fishing and hopefully "catching".

Other than a few small Snapper, a couple of undersized grouper, an illegal Redfish and a small Shark, nothing was caught in the next few hours. So, as the Sun begin to sink slowly in the West, we grabbed a quick bite to eat and knowing the Sow Snapper and Grouper move out from the rigs at night, we got our heavier tackle ready to do some serious night fishing. We baited up a couple of rigs with a live Croaker and a large "Killer Bee" Squid. A couple of other rigs with a real assortment of good old dead bait, consisting of a chunk of fresh cut bait, dead shrimp, Squid, and even a dead menhaden hanging on the tip. Sometimes this will end up attracting Shark, Catfish or small trash fish, however I have caught large, hungry Grouper that just happen to find this an attractive meal.

Not too long after darkness had set in, Steve Stewart was checking the bait on one of the free-lines when all at once the line tightened and we yelled for him to "set the hook"! When he did, it almost jerked the rod out of his hands and he yelled for help from his Dad as the line was fast disappearing and the drag was screaming in protest. Big Steve quickly started the engines and then ran to the bow of the boat to release us from the rig as Terry and I reeled in the three remaining lines so we could follow the fish. "Little Steve was still yelling to his Dad for help, as we slowly motored following the fast moving fish. However, Terry just yelled back for him to hang on and REEL! We each made a guess. What could it be, a big ole' Amberjack, a King, a Shark or even a toothy Barracuda? By the time we had moved some 50 yards from the rig and still not gaining any line, little Steve was so excited, he couldn't say anything but, "Please don't get off what ever you are! Please God, make him hang on"! For the next ten minutes we just kept a tight line and followed the fish away from the rig with little Steve gaining a little line now and then, only to have the fish rip of at least as much as he had gained. After over twenty minutes of Steve hanging on for dear life and between puffing and grunting, he gained on the fish as it sounded and went down to near the bottom. By this time, Steve Stewart was really tired and even offered to have his Dad crank for a while, but Terry turned a deaf ear and told him that no one would touch that rod as this was "His" fish!! I think that a couple of time we thought that we even heard him praying that the fish would give up. One time he even said if it was Shark, to just cut the line as he was worn out. But, he really didn't mean it, for as I approached him with my knife. He gave me a terrified look and said, "No! No! It might not be a Shark! It might be a world record "something"!

"But what ever it is, it's mine! So, we just sat back and watched with silly grins on our face.

Each time that he would stop pumping and or stop taking in line, we would yell at him and remind him that every time he rests the fish rests too, and that We were getting tired of watching him and us not getting to fish. With that he started to pump and wind, pump and wind and finally a huge shape begin to show. Soon the body of a Hammerhead Shark looking to be over eight feet long appeared beside the boat. I did not hesitate to give Mr. Hammerhead a real "Lead head-ache" with my little 38 Magnum Shark Killer. While still quivering, but quite dead, Big Steve and Terry quickly hog-tied the lifeless monster to the boat as I begin to idle back to the now distant rig. I looked over at little Steve and was not sure just who had whipped who in that battle, although, a faint smile finally appeared through the pain. Then he proudly exclaimed, "Wow! That's the biggest fish I have ever caught in my Whole life! !" "Do you think he will win something at the Rodeo'?"

The remainder of the night was somewhat uneventful after that. We each took little "catnaps" with an occasional, but welcome interruption, when one of us caught a fish. We did catch a few nice Snapper and one Grouper, plus several, small Shark and a nasty Barracuda, but nothing to really brag about. I, for one, was pleased to see the morning sun come peaking through, as we started for home and more fun fishing on the way. I noted however, that the seas had gotten a little rougher, but being out of the South, would make the trip easier. We stopped along the way to check out a few rigs and cast a time or two at any anchored shrimp boats, adding a nice Cobia to our catch.

Finally, several hours later, with the boat firmly on the trailer, we headed to the rodeo located on the western shores of the Ocean Springs Beach. Having slept most of the trip back, Steve Stewart was up and back to his normal wide-eyed self and somewhat optimistic about his Shark and had hopes of his nice Jack also placing. Well, the Jack did end up as the third largest of the day, but no prize. But the Shark was by far the largest of the day and therefore a day prize-winner. But, as luck would have it, by the end of the Rodeo, his Jack did not win anything, but his great Hammerhead Shark did place third behind two other Sharks. However, there was only one prize just for the largest Shark. But, the thrill of catching the biggest fish he had ever caught and just the "Taming of the Shark" will always be a winner in the mind of the young teen-age fisherman. And as I always say, it's sure great fun to take a kid fishing.

THE "EDGE"

Most Gulf Coast anglers agree that saltwater fishing offers a "tad-bit" more of the unknown and excitement then freshwater angling. However, that's not to take away the thrill of a big ol' "bucket-mouthed" bass, breaking water as it attacks your top-water lure or the sudden adrenalin flow when a Great Lakes "Caho" nails a deep running down-rigger trolled bait, after hours of "no-action". Yes, when you're fishing saltwater, you don't always know what you might have hooked into. In many cases, you may know what it "might" be, based on the territory your fishing and the bait you are using. But, there are also times when fishing in-shore for smaller game fish, such as Specks, White Trout or even slot-sized Redfish and along comes a big ol' Jack, Shark, Bull Red, Spanish Mackerel or Black Drum. Your line shoots out like you hooked a rocket! You hang on for dear life, not knowing who has who or what's on the other end. Yep! That's the time that you need the "Edge", the need for serious saltwater tackle to give you the edge. I didn't say you need a "Broom-stick and a Winch, just good ol' reliable fish'n gear that matches the species your fishing for, plus a little more. And, if you play your cards, ah I mean "fish" right, you can land the "Big One" on fairly light tackle.

There are times when working your favorite lure over your favorite "hot-spot", you may feel a solid tap that gives your heart a jump. Then, another tap and the adrenalin starts to flow as you drop the rod tip, take up the slack and set the hook; Got him! But what? He's off on a drag-screaming run and just as suddenly, the line goes slack and he's in a mad run back, directly for the boat. You have to reel in the slack as fast as you can, but Mister Fish is moving faster than you can crank. Next thing you know, he's past the boat and taken up the slack so fast he either jerks the hook out of his mouth or snap the light leader line. Always check your drag. You now have another story about "the big one that got away". But a good reel, adequate test line and drag, are not the only thing that will help to determine if you win or loose your fight. A fairly light weight, maybe graphite composite rod, matched with that perfect fast reel will

173

certainly improve your chances. When fishing near or over submerged wrecks or reefs, the hooked fish attempts to run for safe cover, which many times results in a break-off or cut line. Here again, knowing your equipment and how much pressure you can apply to control the fish, yet not to the breaking point, only comes with experience. But, even in a long fight, which you give a little and take a little to keep the fish out of the wreck, can really test the drag system and drag washers that keep the reel cool and working with you. So, in short, you get what you pay for. There's no doubt that the difference between success and failure is many times, in the quality of the fishing gear and therefore the "edge" is in your hands.

YOU GOT TO HAVE FAITH

Rain, rain and more rain! Pouring down rain and the windswept seas prevailed the entire week prior to the 55th Annual Mississippi Deep Sea Fishing Rodeo. The local TV station and the national weather bureau forecasted the rain to continue over the 4th of July Weekend. Really looking bad for the home team, as this is one of the biggest fishing tournaments in the entire state. But, the "Wilson's Fishing Team" still kept the faith and early in the Week, decided that come rain or shine, we were fishing this annual rodeo. After all, we had fished through Hurricane Bertha and fought 10 to 12 foot seas and survived. Why back off for a little rain? Right?

So, come Thursday morning, my two sons, Steve and Marty, plus our guest member, Glenn Bremenkamp, and yours Truly, headed south at 8AM on board the family vessel, "My Reel Mistress". Fully loaded with tackle, ice, bait, food, drinks and all the necessities for a two day, over night fishing trip to the oilrigs. The Sun was trying to peak through the early morning haze. No rain and calm seas and lots of faith. Spirits were high. What more could one ask for other that a great catch. As we traveled south, the water was a little choppy, but after an uneventful three hours of running, we "hooked up" to one of our favorite oilrigs located in over 250 feet of beautiful, clear blue-green water. We kept our eye out for the building thunderstorms as we rigged for fishing, as the Seas now had picked up about a three foot swell. But, "YOU GOT TO HAVE FAITH". Within a few minutes, the wind did come and the white caps did show. The rain came and this went on for over an hour, but fortunately, we had prepared for rain and on came the little yellow rain suits. We still got wet from the warm, wind-driven rain, however we continued to bait up and fish and within a few minutes, Marty hooked up with our first Amberjack. Spirits rose and faith was renewed. But before anyone else even got a bite, Marty was back on the bottom and was cranking in another fish! This time, it was a smaller "A.J." Since we could only keep one per person, this one became our first "catch and release", as it was way too early in the trip to keep a small one and we had faith the next three would be much bigger. But, the waves were increasing as the winds raged, and no more bites for the next thirty minutes.

Just about the time that our faith was at a standstill, the wind started to let up a bit, and our guest angler, Glenn, let out a loud grunt, as he set the hook and started cranking like crazy. It did not take long for the lanky six-foot, two hundred plus pound former Vietnam "FAC" pilot to put the first nice Red Snapper in the boat. Hey!! Faith was back as strong as ever. We did kid him a little about being lucky however, during the trip, Glenn caught four of the biggest Snapper. Later in the afternoon, he set the hook so hard that he even broke one of the heavyduty rods. We suggested that he change to a "circle hook" and let the fish hook themselves. That might save another rod, plus it usually did not injure small fish that could be released, basically unharmed. Normally, the hook catches the fish in the corner of the mouth. (This was before it was a Federal law that one must use a circle hook in Federal waters when using natural bait. Live or dead)

By late afternoon, the rain clouds were gone and the sun was trying to make a final appearance on the Western horizon as we prepared for night fishing before it got dark. We had several nice Snapper in the cooler, plus a couple of 35 to 40 pound Cobia. Several Arnberjack were released after we had our limit as well as dozens of small Snapper. We stopped counting the number of Shark released in the 10 to 50 pound range. So, already we had caught lots of fish, but had faith that more great fishing was ahead. After a quick snack for our evening meal, we got seriously busy getting ready for some "real" fishing. The heavier rods were rigged, a couple of free lines were baited up with live bait to let out behind the boat and we were in business as night was upon us. Much to our dislike, Shark were the most frequent bite for the first hour or two, however, by about 10pm, things picked up. Actually, Glenn went to work and for the next hour, out fished us all. First he caught two of his four "Sow Snappers". Then a beautiful big "Chub". He was using a big old True Temper broomstick, but he had the right feel and certainly had the "Faith"!

As the evening progressed, lots of fish were caught and several were lost. (for one reason or another) But the main thing was that everyone caught all kinds of fish. It seemed like someone was "catching" every few minutes. I did get bored a couple of times after bite after bite of small fish or catching trash fish or illegal Snapper. So I just left my bait on the bottom and waited until something really big came along. When I did finally reel in, I was surprised to find a nasty tempered Moray Eel on the hook. Upon a close look, Steve, Marty and I agreed that it was unusual looking and that we would take it in to our marine biologist friend, "Buck" Buchanan and have him identify it. You never know when fishing at two, three or four hundred feet, all sorts of marine life may be there and we have caught several state records at these depths. So, into the bucket it went. It was not long before I caught another one, and this time a different species. In to the bucket it went. (We did find out later that the first one was a Black Tail Moray and the second one was a Purple Mouth Moray Eel. There must have been a coral bed or some type of underwater structure right under where I was fishing, as the very next time my bait hit the bottom, I felt a small tug and brought in another smaller Eel. Just as it cleared the side of the boat it dropped off the hook and fell to the floor. Before I could move it had latched its' tiny, needle-sharp teeth into my middle toe and hung on, no matter how hard I shook my foot, I yelped, screamed, hollered and finally jerked it off my toe, but not before it had penetrated a hundred pin holes and then made a deep gash across my toe. I am here to tell you, do everything you can to avoid getting bit by a Moray Eel, even if you have to wear boots, sit on a chair with your feet up or even jump overboard. I have been stuck well over a hundred times by a Hardhead Catfish, nicked by the barb of Sting Rays and stung by all sorts of bees, hornets, ants and spiders, but never in my life have I felt the stinging pain that the bite of that Eel gave me. It was several hours before the searing pain stopped and it did not stay locally in the toe area. During the next 30 minutes it moved all the way up my leg. Well, enough of that, but by the way, both Eels turned out to be State records for hook and line and at the time the Purple Mouth Eel was a pending all tackle World record. Yep. You got to have faith no matter what the pain.

In the meantime, the fishing really slowed down, even the Sharks took a rest, but not Marty and Steve. They just kept fish'n away and periodically put a nice fish in the boat. After a quick nap, Glenn was back reeling and grunt'n as he landed another nice 14 or 15 pound Snapper.

However, the early morning hours also brought bigger waves and the fish seemed to stop biting completely. So, we caught a few Z's until at the crack of dawn and we all seemed to wake up about the same time. It was stormy all around us so we figured our fishing time was short. We unhooked from the rig and moved slowly around the rig to an area that we had caught A.J.s before. As we moved around the corner of the rig Marty dropped a live Hardtail behind the boat and let it sink. He immediately hooked up and we expedited a departure

from the rig. After about a 15 minute fight, Steve gaffed a nice 30 pounder. Well, that made three and we still had were allowed one more, so Steve volunteered and we headed back to the corner of the rig for another shot. We had seen A.J _ that were pushing 100 pounds around this rig on previous trips.

Just as we were again departing the corner of the rig, Steve felt a couple of light bumps and started letting out line. At about fifty feet from the rig, feeling a heavy weight, he set the hook and the fight was on. This time it was obvious that the fish was much larger than the other three and it looked like it was trying to pull Steve out of the boat. Yes, again, faith soured. This could be a Rodeo winner. After about twenty minutes, it appeared that the fish was starting to give line. Shortly there after, he felt dead weight and begin to reel like crazy, hoping that his prize had not gotten off. As his huge catch hit the surface, a cry of joy came from all of us. It looked like one of the big boys that we had seen on previous trips. Marty made a perfect gaff and Steve grabbed the tail of the fish and on board it came. "High-Fives" were in order and everyone was in high spirits. We really had the faith now. Well, just about that time, Mother Nature let us know that she was still around, as a blinding flash of lightening, followed by a loud clap of thunder quickly brought us back to reality. We iced the fish, stowed the fishing equipment and headed north. Fortunately, we had falling seas and were able to stay ahead of the storm, even as the seas were building to 5 to 6 footers. But things got worse. About halfway home, the Port engine let out an alarming squeal. We immediately shut down the bad engine and checked to see just what was the problem.

After confirming that we had a broken belt, which runs several essential parts of the engine, we proceeded on with just the Starboard engine. Making between 8 to 10 knots until we were about 20 miles from "Dog Key Pass at Horn Island and the Starboard engine started acting up and soon dropped down to just idle speed. Therefore even a slower trip the rest of the way home. To make a long story short, we arrived at Ocean Springs Small Craft Harbor just nine and a half hours from the time we departed the rig. But, the story does not end here. Stay tuned. You got to have faith. Remember, our boat trailer was on up the Bay at the D'Iberville Boat launch under the I 1-10 bridge. We could not locate any of our friends at home so Glenn called his wife, Ann and she came to Ocean Springs and took Glenn and Steve to go get the trailer. Since the weigh in closed at 8pm, we thought we could still make it down the highway to Gulfport and make it. At shortly after 7pm, with the boat on the trailer and in tow, we headed down the Ocean Springs Beach toward highway 90. Still had the faith.

Just in front of the Ocean Springs Yacht Club, there is a sharp right turn to the East and several cars were coming in the opposite direction so I stopped to let them make the turn first. Well the first car stopped short and motioned for us to come ahead so I could make the wide turn. But I had not pulled over far enough left to clear the comer curb on the right, which had a sharp, protruding edge. You guess it. It punched a big hole in my right front trailer tire. Now what? (Gotta keep the faith!) But making the scales tonight was out of the question. Being the 4th of July, the traffic was really bad and even though I did have a spare trailer tire, it was at home. Fortunately Glenn was still right behind us in his car and we headed for the house. Within about 45 minutes, we were back, changed the tire and heading back to the house. By this time, everyone was straining to keep the faith, but with two broke engines, our fishing was over for this rodeo.

But all's well, that ends well. Other than having two broken outboard engines, a punctured boat trailer tire, a very sore toe and not being able to fish the last day ofthe Rodeo, we all still enjoyed catching a lot of fish and the comradery. During the award ceremony on Sunday night, Marty presented his 'Speckled Trout" fish print to Mr. Ted Jones for him to award to the first place Speckled Trout winner in tribute to his son, the late, "Rick" Jones, for which there was a special dedication at this years rodeo. Rick was also the brother to the current Sun Herald Sports Editor, "Al" Jones. As for the Wilson Boys and Glenn, our faith paid off. Steve's A.J weighed 78 pounds, 9 ounces and won first place. I ended up with 3 state records, one was a pending world record. This brought our family total to 13 state records and 1 world record with 3 pending. Not a bad trip, considering the obstacles we overcame. Oh yea, I was surprised and honored at the awards ceremony, as I was awarded the "Sport Fisherman of the Year" Yep! "You Got To Have Faith!"

A SALTY COOK

I will always remember Christmas of 1994. It was not just another great family day when the birth of Christ is celebrated and Santa is on every child's lips as their eyes fly open on Christmas morning. It started out very early that morning; when the phone awakened me about three a.m. It was the wife of a very close friend and old fishing buddy and she quickly advised me that the Doctor at Keesler Medical Center had called her and stated that her husband was not doing well and had ask for her. Within the hour we were at his bedside, however by then, even as he struggled for every breath, he was in a deep sleep and never woke up.

Well, my old fish'n buddy, that weathered old salt, Grady Cook, didn't make it through the morning, and if there is a, for sure, "happy fishing ground", that's where he be today. Grady Cook was a fish'n legend and many years of his life was spent participating in his favorite sport. He loved to share this great hobby with his friends, especially his little friends. It seems like just yesterday that Grady and my grandson, Blake, would sit, fishing side by side, every time the three of us went fishing together. Blake, so intent on catching fish that he would seldom take time out to eat or drink anything and Grady, was paying more attention to Blake catch'n fish then wetting a line himself. I used to marvel, in that even though Grady was a chain smoker, he seldom lit up when he was fishing with Blake. He was always talk'n to Blake in a soft, quiet voice, with words of instruction each time that Blake would hook into a fish. "That's a boy, let him run a little." or "O.K. now, tight'n down on him a little" or "Bring him on in son, that fish belong to you." Brady loved to work with the kids when it came to learn'n to fish.

I often remember from the many years of fishing together, the little quips that this old fisherman would come up with that seemed appropriate for the occasion. Most of which, however, I could not quote in mixed company, but I do have to admit, that in a man's world, he always got a laugh. I remember one early morning, just as the light of a new day was creeping over the horizon, we had dropped anchor at the deep rock pile north of Ship Island and Grady was trying to re-rig his line for bottom fishing. After three or four attempts to thread the hook in the dim, early morning light, he enlightened us with one of his neat vernacular words and said in a disgusted voice, "This is harder than trying to put a straight jacket on a bobcat in a telephone booth!!" And, of course, anyone that has ever fished very much with my late friend, Grady Cook, no doubt can recall him saying, "Well, sometimes it's chicken; sometimes it's feathers, and sometimes it's just plain chicken S—!" But then he'd smile and chuckle, and say, "But even when I don't catch a fish, I do enjoy the company . . . Thank you." And he did!!

A few days after Grady passed away, another fishing buddy of ours, John Lambeth, former Outdoors Editor of the Sun Herald, wrote a three column epitaph about Grady and the many years that the three of us had fished together. Let me tell you that we did catch our share. As John said in his article, "We ate a few feathers' but we had our fun with the chickens too." We could tell you many a story about weathering rough seas and the wind and rain that can spoil your whole day. During the past ten years, I have written several stories about fishing trips that Grady Cook and I have shared, the good and the bad. One trip in particular, I will never forget and we never even got the boat launched.

About four or five years ago, Grady and I got an early start one morning to Pearl River. I mean, we had boat loaded, live bait on board and was darn near to our turn off of I-10 to Pearlington, when we ran smack into a fog bank. At the time we weren't really all that concerned, as we just slowed down to a comfortable speed and headed for our boat launch just beyond the bridge on old "90". Well, as we were waiting to turn off the highway to the boat launch, we got hit in the rear end by a truck that was going a way too fast in the fog. Should'a both been killed or at least injured, but the boat and trailer saved us. The boat was a 14 root blazer and it flew over the top or the car. The trailer squashed like an accordion, absorbing the major part of the impact. Once again, ole' Grady had a vernacular response, however, at the time, I found it quite appropriate. Yes, Grady Cook was an old salty. A grand old, man of the seas. Granted, he could hug you to death sometimes with his endless chatter about what ever his favorite disfavor was, but the majority or the time, he was one great fish'n buddy. He loved the water, to fish, to show and tell someone how and where to fish, to rig a line, to bait a hook or how to play a fish. During his 68 years of fishing and catching, Grady learned a bunch and was always quick to share. Grady Cook taught all of us a few things about fishing and even about being a friend.

Grady will he missed in this world, by me, by my grandson, Blake, by his wife, Marie, by his family and by the many other fishermen that knew Grady as their friend. Although I am saddened at the loss, I also feel fortunate to have known each a friend and fishing buddy. I'm confident the Lord welcomed and blessed our Grady Cook, into his "Happy Fishing Ground."

AUTOBIOGRAPHY

Lieutenant Colonel, Dick E. Wilson, USAF Retired, was born and raised on the beautiful lakes of northern Indiana. He was a graduate of Indiana University, with a B.S. degree and commissioned as a 2nd Lieutenant. He completed pilot training and accumulated over 6,000 hours flying fighter and training type aircraft, including over 360 combat missions in Viet Nam. Following retirement, in 1976, from Keesler Air Force Base, Colonel Wilson owned and operated Wilson Fishing Camp until 1988 and worked for the City of Biloxi until final retirement in 1997. He has continued to be very active as a volunteer in State, County and municipal activities and organizations. An avid fisherman and marine conservationist, Colonel Wilson enjoys writing real life fishing stories.